Sacred Strangers

What the Bible's Outsiders Can Teach Christians

Nancy Haught

LITURGICAL PRESS

Collegeville, Minnesota

www.litpress.org

Cover design by Amy Marc. Illustration courtesy of Wikimedia Commons.

Library of Congress Cataloging-in-Publication Data

Names: Haught, Nancy, author.
Title: Sacred strangers : what the Bible's outsiders can teach Christians / Nancy Haught.
Description: Collegeville, Minnesota : Liturgical Press, 2017. | Includes bibliographical references.
Identifiers: LCCN 2017035676 (print) | LCCN 2017017081 (ebook) | ISBN 9780814645291 (ebook) | ISBN 9780814645048
Subjects: LCSH: Strangers—Religious aspects—Christianity. | Strangers in the Bible.
Classification: LCC BR115.S73 (print) | LCC BR115.S73 H38 2017 (ebook) | DDC 220.9/2—dc23
LC record available at https://lccn.loc.gov/2017035676

"Through biblical stories and careful exegesis, Nancy Haught shows how God's abundant grace is oftentimes present and active where we least expect it: in the outsiders, the marginalized, the strangers in the land. By re-examining familiar stories and lesser-known characters in the Bible, Haught confirms the words of St. Paul that 'God chose the lowly and despised, those who count for nothing,' to bring God's revelation and truth 'to those who count for something' (1 Cor 1:28). Beautifully written in a clear, engaging, and poetic style, *Sacred Strangers* will inspire the reader to look beyond religious and societal stereotypes to see how God's abiding love creates prophets and saviors, even in 'the least' among us. We need this book now more than ever."

— Msgr. Patrick S. Brennan
Pastor, St. Mary's Cathedral, Portland, Oregon

"*Sacred Strangers* reminds us that God cares for and protects the very people whom we identify as foreign and suspect. Through careful examination of several Bible stories about those 'other' people, *Sacred Strangers* shows us that these outsiders are both blessed by God and used by God to carry out God's work in the world. This book is a timely antidote against xenophobia and religious intolerance: the people whom we push away and exclude may be God's messengers and part of God's divine plan. This book is an excellent resource for group and individual Bible study, preachers and teachers, or anybody who wants to more fully appreciate the mysterious ways God works in our lives."

— The Rev. Sarah Coakley Lewis, pastor
Piedmont Presbyterian Church, Portland, Oregon

"Nancy Haught's fresh *Sacred Strangers* is a brilliant conversation with the rest of us about unsung role models in the Bible. Haught makes the case that people we hardly know in Scripture—or in our lives today— could light our paths and elevate humanity in the twenty-first century. Prepare for delicious prose, insight, and inspiration."

— Joann Byrd, longtime newspaper reporter, editor, and former
Pulitzer Prize board member, author

"In an age in which the stranger is distrusted and rejected, Haught's book calls Christians to explore the rich spiritual gifts awaiting them from 'the other.' *Sacred Strangers* is not only pertinent—it is a necessary compass in these trying times."

—Rev. Dr. Marilyn Sewell
 Minister Emerita
 First Unitarian Church, Portland, Oregon

"'Strangers mystify us,' Nancy Haught writes, yet they help us learn about ourselves, our beliefs, and our world—and for these reasons they are people to engage, not fear and reject. With clarity, insight, and skill, Haught convincingly shows how the Bible compels Christians to enter relationship and dialogue with those of other faiths and beliefs. This book is a much-needed contribution to interfaith and cross-cultural understanding in a time of deepening division."

—Tom Krattenmaker
 USA Today contributing columnist
 Author, *Confessions of a Secular Jesus Follower*

"Reading *Sacred Strangers* is like hearing six inspiring homilies, attending an uplifting retreat, and learning from your favorite Scripture professor all at the same time. Haught has the ability to make Scripture come alive as she weaves the scholarly with the practical. There has never been a more important time for a book like *Sacred Strangers*. The discussion questions are excellent. I can't wait to use this book with our parents and faculty."

—Patricia Gorman
 Theology Department Chairperson
 St. Mary's Academy, Portland, Oregon

For Freddy, who always believed I had a book in me.

Contents

Preface

Not long ago, I reached for my Bible. The worn, blue, cloth-covered book had seen me through seminary twenty-five years ago. It had sustained me through years of teaching high school and college religion courses. It had spurred my daily newspaper reporting on religion for decades. But on this particular day, the frayed binding slipped from my fingers. Holy Scripture landed face down on the floor. Inwardly, I cringed, remembering a seminary professor who was scandalized by how casually some of his students treated our copies of the Bible. Outwardly, I bent to pick up the slips of paper that had scattered across the rug:

> My beloved husband's handwritten note left on the day I graduated from seminary.
>
> The outline of a long-ago talk about why I love the Old Testament.
>
> A yellowing, folded copy of my wedding vows—typed thirty-three years ago.
>
> And a *New Yorker* cartoon that I read again that day for the thousandth time. A man and a woman sit in their living room. "I'm sorry, dear. I wasn't listening," she says to him. "Could you repeat what you've said since we've been married?"

As I gathered up the scraps that have been stuck in my Bible for years, I thought about why I keep them between its covers. These bits and pieces from my life remind me that the Bible *is* what they *are*:

A handwritten love letter.
A declaration of devotion.
A promise for the future.
And one side of a conversation that I have not always heard.

Like pottery shards displayed in a museum, these scattered bits and pieces are artifacts that reflect my attitude toward Scripture. I do not believe that every word in the Bible was spoken by God. Or that the stories within it are factual. I do believe that the Bible contains truth that careful readings can reveal. I also believe that careful readings are hard to come by in our world today. They require background and context. Very often, they overturn our preconceptions. A careful reading takes into account history, sociology, anthropology, psychology, rhetoric, and style—at the very least. It's a daunting task to sift through so much material in search of the meaning, or even *a* meaning, buried in a biblical text.

Meaning. There's the rub. It's folly, I think, to assume that a particular Bible passage has only one meaning. A good *New Yorker* cartoon carries many different meanings. So it can be hard to know with any certainty what a handful of lines from the Bible might have meant to the person who wrote them or read them or heard them for the first time. Let alone what those same lines may mean to us now, generations later. Sometimes it's easier to read past difficult passages or rely on someone else to do the scholarship and decode the message for us. We all do that from time to time. But when we skip passages or rely on others' interpretations, however well meant they may be, we may overlook a sliver of truth. An insight that could inspire and support our faith and enrich our lives.

We live in a difficult world. As I write, the United States is at war against terrorism and wary of countries that may be on the brink of nuclear weaponry. Refugees from the Middle East and Africa are flooding Europe and making their way more slowly into the United States. Immigration, whether it is illegal or not, is a political issue as Americans worry about the loss of jobs, the struggle to fund education, and the growth of the federal budget. The gap between rich and poor widens and the middle class shrinks. Mass shootings and fatal encounters with police begin to seem commonplace. Religion is not a refuge. People of faith are at odds over gay marriage, abortion, the death penalty, and refugees. Whatever we believe or don't believe about God, we are all surrounded by fear, mistrust, even hatred of people whose religious beliefs are different from our own. The notion of "religious tolerance" seems almost quaint. An old-fashioned phrase that sounds, in theory, like a good idea, but breaks down in practice.

But before we Christians surrender to these trying times, consider one truth that runs through the Bible, one we often overlook: Scripture is shot through with stories of "outsiders" who know God better than the "insiders." By insiders, I mean the Hebrews or the Israelites or the Jews or the followers of Jesus, the people who usually believe that they occupy God's inner circle, the ones we modern readers identify with when we read the Bible. When we consider these stories carefully, they remind those of us on the inside that we have much to learn from those on the outside. Strangers—the "others" whom we suspect, fear, distrust, dismiss, even damn—may be sacred. They may be living examples of holiness that we need to survive, even thrive, in a world where violence aims to separate us and mire us all in despair. Strangers become our teachers, if we are willing to pay attention.

Acknowledgments

I've thought about this book for a long time, and many people have helped me see it through. I am indebted to my writing group, Peggy McMullen, JoLene Krawczak, and David Stabler, who read bits and pieces over and over, always with encouragement; to three of my teachers, Gina Hens-Piazza, Patricia Gorman, and Msgr. Patrick S. Brennan, who helped me appreciate the power of Scripture; to my first editor and dear friend, Joann Byrd; to the Rev. Sarah Coakley Lewis, an early reader with good suggestions; to Ed and Dawn Kropp, who lent me their lovely beach house so I could write in a beautiful place; to my friend Faiza Noor; and to my beloved sons, Ante and Nels Vulin, who took this project seriously and spurred me on when I needed it, and to their beautiful wives, Emily Kropp and Ashley Vulin, who inspire me in their own ways and to whom I have entrusted my greatest treasure. All the mistakes in this manuscript are mine.

Introduction
Me First

Faiza and I made quick work of the Thanksgiving program for our Muslim-Christian dialogue group. We decided to ask students and adults from each tradition to talk briefly about what they'd gained by knowing each other. Once we'd decided who to ask and nailed down the program details, we relaxed over our coffee at Starbucks. She talked about her daughters' school and the challenges of being a part-time university student herself. I remembered my own experience, juggling children and seminary studies—taking the time to sew Halloween costumes the night before my first Hebrew exam. I sympathized with Faiza. And I joked about being newly retired and facing an opposite challenge—having too much time on my hands.

But religion is what had brought the two of us together in the first place, so our small talk soon turned to more spiritual matters. Faiza, who is Muslim, had been attending a Christian Bible study. Her presence made it a "nontraditional" Bible study, she quipped. But all the women were united in their efforts to grow closer to God, she said. Over time, she had listened intently to the women's prayers. She was surprised that their petitions were so specific and that they spoke with confidence that God would do what they had asked. Their prayers cut to the heart of the matter and didn't include much in the way of thanksgiving or praise. In her own experience of Islam, thanksgiving and praise are the heart of prayer, she said. Prayers often quote passages from the Qur'an, the sacred book of

Islam. Personal requests may be rare in public. Faiza thought of prayer as a general call for help, strength, or blessing.

Driving home, I thought about my own prayer practice, how it had changed over the years. In high school, I'd prayed that the Jell-O I'd made would set up before dinner. Later, when my husband was fighting cancer, I prayed the name of Jesus, over and over and over. I couldn't find words to encompass Fred's suffering—or ours. I could not think of what to ask. Was miraculous healing out of the question? What was fair, given all the suffering in the world? What was faithful, given what we believed? We human beings don't always know how God would work in a particular set of circumstances. As I turned into my driveway, I thought about the role of confidence in prayer and the danger of thinking that when God doesn't respond in the way we desire, it means the prayer is unanswered. Those thoughts stayed with me all that day and a year later they come back to me from time to time. Along with gratitude that a brief conversation with someone from another faith tradition helped me reflect on my own religious practice.

In thirty years as a newspaper reporter writing about religion, I had these encounters all the time. For most of those years, I loved my job. Religion was fascinating to me and, as a person of faith myself, I was curious about other people's experiences. At the same time, it was often daunting to reach out to strangers, to ask them to share their deepest beliefs so I could reduce them to print for other strangers to read in a daily paper. But, to my unending surprise, people did agree to talk to me. And often, not always I will admit, but often I came away with more than a story to file on deadline. I came away with a clearer understanding of my own faith and a greater appreciation of a person who had once been a stranger. I retired in 2013 and, apart from the people I used to work with, it is these encounters with strangers that I miss the most. Now I have to be intentional about seeking them out—so I joined the Christian-Muslim group, where I met Faiza.

In the process of creating these opportunities for myself, I've thought about the role of strangers or outsiders in the Bible. In both Old and New Testament stories, outsiders come from other countries, cultures, or regions. They worship other gods. They have been or are enemies or rivals. They may have political power or wealth. They may be poor or sick. They are all met with a certain amount of distrust, even outright fear. Stranger danger is not a new idea. But within these biblical stories, it's often the strangers who embody the true characteristics of faith, truer than those of the Hebrews, Israelites, Jews, or followers of Jesus that they meet. As insiders ourselves, we need to pay more attention to the examples of outsiders.

Strangers mystify us, but they help us figure out who we are. We human beings define ourselves according to the groups we belong to, and we categorize people outside those groups as "others" or "outsiders." Depending on the circumstances, we separate ourselves into larger and smaller groups: We are Americans. We are members of the upper class, the middle class, or the working poor. We are Democrats, or Republicans, or independent voters, or we don't vote at all. We are Christians, or Evangelicals, or Catholics. As insiders in these circles, we sometimes assume that outsiders are ignorant, hostile, envious, eager to steal or destroy whatever it is we insiders value. We think outsiders are less moral, less thoughtful, and more conniving than we are. When the circle is a religious one, we insiders assume that outsiders are gullible, less faithful than we are, or altogether faithless. Too often we keep our distance out of fear, convenience, a sense of superiority, even ignorance of the outsiders themselves. It's easier to criticize them and elevate ourselves if we don't know much about them or don't think critically about ourselves. We focus on differences, real or imagined, and perceive them as obstacles. We are wary of finding common ground—if we believe that it exists at all. We see evidence of these non-relationships all around us: within our families, communities, countries, religions. But if we are Christians,[1] who value the Bible and its insights,[2] we cannot afford to ignore the biblical stories in which strangers become sacred examples of how to live a holy life. We need to read the stories in which strangers redirect us to the path we thought we had been following all along.

The notion of hospitality to strangers is central to both the Old and New Testaments. It is a principle that is sometimes repeated as a simple admonition or command. Moses reminds the Israelites, in Deuteronomy 10:19, "You shall also love the stranger, for you were strangers in the land of Egypt." Later, the Christian Letter to the Hebrews (13:2) warns us, "Do not neglect to show hospitality to strangers, for by doing that some have entertained angels without knowing it." While it may be easy to forget or ignore such scattered words of advice, the value of strangers is a steady undercurrent throughout Scripture. In these stories, strangers can come alive for us and, perhaps, live longer in our hearts and minds than a simple command. I've chosen half a dozen biblical stories to explore line by line, some with strangers whose names we don't remember or never knew: the magi, whose gifts amounted to more than frankincense, gold, and myrrh; Hagar, an Egyptian slave who named God; Rahab, a hooker (or an honest innkeeper) who did what it took to protect her family; Naaman, an enemy general who listened to slaves and servants; the Samaritan woman at the well, who became the first woman preacher; and the Syrophoenician woman, who argued with Jesus and won. There are many others, many of them more famous than some of the passages I have chosen. The story of Ruth comes immediately to mind. Or the Good Samaritan of Jesus' parable. But sometimes, unfamiliarity encourages new understanding, so I've chosen some lesser-known passages. I've relied on the work of scholars, teachers, and pastors I have known or whose work I've read. I've suggested questions for group discussion or private reflection. Endnotes and a bibliography will help readers who want to know more. I've used the New Revised Standard Version of the Bible (yes, the tattered copy I dropped at the beginning of this book) for sentimental and scholarly reasons.[3] From here on out, I'll refer to the Old Testament as the Hebrew Bible, the New Testament as Christian Scripture. (I learned in seminary that calling the testaments old and new implied judgments I didn't intend.) And, finally, for the sake of this work, I'll refer to the four gospels by their traditional names, even though many scholars agree that they are the work of other hands.

It is my hope that reading and thinking about these stories will remind me and encourage readers to seek out strangers, or at least take advantage of the opportunities that life in our diverse country and world offers. My own example, my relationship with Faiza, is a personal one, a minor one, given what is going on in the world today. Religion not only separates people, but it has become the root cause of unspeakable violence. Extremists wage war within and across national boundaries. In addition to the men, women, and children they starve, torture, and kill, these extremists are attacking, or trying to attack, long-held religious convictions that have cultivated peace in times past. One way to thwart the extremist effort is for ordinary people of faith to live out the religious values at the core of their respective traditions. To forge relationships that fly in the face of extremist arguments and challenge their superficial and selfish agendas. To talk about these experiences and urge others to undertake them, too.

It is not easy work. Sometimes these encounters are awkward, uncomfortable, or troubling. In some cases, there may not be much, if any, common ground to stand on. An honest meeting with a stranger may force us to focus on our own failings. But other conversations may be relaxed, thought-provoking, and encouraging. Stilted or smooth, these discussions teach us lessons about ourselves, our faith, other people and their faith. Religion can separate people, but it can bring them together—as it did for Faiza and me. And I believe that while there is work to be done when people of different faiths meet, there may also be time, if we persist in our efforts, to relax and reflect on our own faith. To see what it is we believe, to search out or recover what's missing, to face the challenges that life brings and love demands.

I

The Magi,
an Unopened Gift
Matthew 2:1-12

After promising in the last chapter to share unfamiliar
Bible stories, here I am beginning with one that we
modern readers think we know inside and out. We've
heard the Christmas story so often that it's easy for us to overlook
its details and miss the significance they carry. For starters, there is
more than one Christmas story. I taught religion for many years, to
high school and college students, and many of them were surprised
to discover that the Bible includes two different versions of Jesus'
birth. In our memories, we often weave the two tales together and
think of them as one story. But reading and thinking about each
story, separately, is a good way to begin reflecting on their original
meanings. And it paves the way for us to think about what the two
passages might mean to us. So, let's begin by asking, who are the
outsiders in these Christmas stories?

Luke tells the story in which shepherds watch over their flocks
and hear the angelic chorus. In chapter 2 of the gospel, verse 10,
"the angel of the Lord" appears to the shepherds and says,

> "Do not be afraid; for see—I am bringing you good news
> of great joy for all the people: to you is born this day in the
> city of David a Savior, who is the Messiah, the Lord."

When the shepherds hear this message, they set out for Bethlehem to see the newborn for themselves. The shepherds are outsiders, of a sort. They may live outdoors, most certainly outside of town, but chances are they're Jewish, like Mary and Joseph and most of the inhabitants of old Bethlehem.[1] The argument can be made that they are insiders.

The real strangers are in Matthew's story, which does not include shepherds or a heavenly host bearing good tidings. In the Gospel of Matthew, the messenger is not an angel but a star, and it rises east of Judea, far from Bethlehem. The men who see the star and interpret its meaning are not Jews, but strangers known as magi. Within the biblical story, they are the first outsiders who search for Jesus, the first to lay eyes on him.[2] It is their first glimpse that opens our eyes to the Son of God. The magi are models of integrity, humility, determination, and courage. Their examples outshine those of King Herod, the chief priests, and the scribes, whose selfish interest and spiritual ignorance have blinded them to the truth. Bible scholar Raymond E. Brown argues that the true significance of the magi's story is far greater than the twelve verses Matthew uses to tell it. The magi embody "the essence of the good news," Brown writes. God becomes present to us as a child whose life will become "salvation to those who had eyes to see."[3] So, what does Brown "see" in this story about strangers? Vision is the first gift of the magi. It is through their eyes that we readers first see Jesus.[4] Their story begins in Matthew 2:1:

> In the time of King Herod, after Jesus was born in Bethlehem
> of Judea, wise men from the East came to Jerusalem.

The Bible doesn't say explicitly how many magi there are, let alone give them names or even specify their nationality. All those supposed details came later, outside of the biblical text, steeped in centuries of tradition,[5] which often fills in the gaps of Scripture. But in the biblical text, the strangers are described in Greek as *magoi* (singular form of the plural *magos*), a difficult word to translate for modern readers. The word itself is used positively and negatively in ancient texts to describe mystics, magicians, or outright frauds.[6] Some translations of the Bible call the strangers in Matthew's story "astrologers."[7] We often think of them as "wise men" without giving much thought to the wisdom they actually possess. The Bible does not elaborate. Some scholars consider the magi less than wise. "They seem to know less about what has happened or about what it may signify than anyone else,"[8] Mark Allan Powell writes in his discussion of Matthew 2. But we will come to our own conclusion. Matthew does not refer to the magi by their nationality (or nationalities, if they are from more than one country).[9] He doesn't call them *Gentiles*, a kind of catch-all word used later in the gospel to refer to non-Jews.[10] Matthew describes these men only by their profession: they are magi.

In the ancient world, magi were sometimes respected professionals, consulted by kings and often acted in service to them. Other times, magi were manipulators or charlatans. But in this context, the writer makes no claim, good or bad, about their profession. We don't have to either. So far, we have the barest of bones to work with: These men come to Jerusalem from the East after the birth of Jesus. Once in the city, they seek out Herod, the ruling king of the Jews, and ask him this question:

> "Where is the child who has been born king of the Jews? For we observed his star at its rising, and have come to pay him homage."

Whether we approve of their profession or not, these magi, at least at this point in time, have made their "science" the focus of their lives.[11] They have gathered intelligence from the natural world—a star—and they act on it, even if it doesn't seem to apply directly to their circumstances. They aren't Jews themselves, but they respect the birth of a ruler when it is proclaimed by a star. They are confident enough in their observation and conclusions that they are willing to travel some distance to acknowledge their own interpretation. They use the phrase "king of the Jews." Brown notes that this is the same phrase that will hang over Jesus' head as he is crucified. It is the only other place outside the stories of Jesus' death and resurrection that the designation is used, Brown writes.[12] It is a title first bestowed by the magi, not by Jesus' own countrymen but by outsiders. The magi go on to use a personal pronoun, referring to the sign they have observed as *his* star. They say they have been aware of the sign since "its rising." They have known of it for at least the time it's taken them to travel to Jerusalem. As is the custom in their time, they associate the star with the birth of an important personage.[13] And they assume that the existing king of the Jews, an insider, probably knows whom they are seeking.

At the same time, the magi don't know everything. They come asking for information. They do not assume or pretend that they are experts, even though they have seen the star early on. And they have a clear idea of what their interpretation of the star's meaning requires of them: They have to find this newborn king and acknowledge his royal birth. They are humble, honest, and willing to ask questions so they can fulfill what they see as their obligation. As outsiders, they're very different from Herod, the insider they are consulting.

> When King Herod heard this, he was frightened, and all Jerusalem with him; and calling together all the chief priests and scribes of the people, he inquired of them where the Messiah was to be born.

Now our focus turns to Herod, the man whom the occupying Romans had appointed to rule over the Jews. Of course, he is afraid when the magi mention another king of the Jews, one "born" into this position.[14] Not only is Herod worried, but so is "all Jerusalem."[15] A ruler's fear is shared by the city's population here at the beginning of Jesus' life. The same will be true at the end. Matthew is laying the groundwork for the entire gospel, which will contrast those people who accept Jesus as the Messiah and those who don't.[16] But the foreshadowing is brief. The passage at hand concentrates on the magi and the answer to their question. The chief priests and scribes, who, we assume, know Scripture and its prophecies well, give Herod an answer:

They told him, "In Bethlehem of Judea; for so it has been written by the prophet:
'And you, Bethlehem, in the land of Judah,
    are by no means least among the rulers of Judah;
for from you shall come a ruler
    who is to shepherd my people Israel.'"

The scribes and chief priests know precisely what the strangers are asking, even though, as religious leaders of the Jews, they don't seem to have taken any action themselves in regard to the prophecy.[17] They repeat it for Herod, who now has a question of his own for the magi:

Then Herod secretly called for the wise men and learned from them the exact time when the star had appeared.

Herod speaks to the magi privately to find out when the birth may have occurred. We can almost hear him doing the math in his head as he plots to kill any child who might turn out to be his newborn rival. Quickly, he enlists the strangers as spies[18] and sends them to Bethlehem, with these instructions:

"Go and search diligently for the child; and when you have found him, bring me word so that I may also go and pay him homage."

Herod asks the magi to "search diligently for the child." He has something more deliberate in mind than a wondrous star shining down on Jesus' birthplace.[19] If we know what's coming, we shudder. He has no desire to "pay homage" to the child. He has evil plans. He does not bother to send anyone with the magi or even have them followed so that he can be sure of killing the right child. He will kill every child born within the last two years. His response to the magi's message that *one* child has been born is to slaughter *many* children. His orders will be sweeping, his violence will be engulfing.

But if we set aside the evil of Herod, if we focus again on the magi and their behavior, we see three things:

The magi are observant, watching and listening openly and honestly. We don't know whether they are suspicious or scornful of Herod. We know only that they hear him out.

They answer his question truthfully. They do not guard their information, even from someone like Herod, whose motives may seem questionable to them.

They pay attention to both natural signs and earthly authorities, to the star and to the acting king of the Jews, to his advisors and to their Jewish Scripture. Later, when the magi choose what or who to follow, they'll do so with their eyes wide open.

After this encounter with Herod, the narrative point of view shifts back to the magi:

> When they had heard the king, they set out; and there, ahead of them, went the star that they had seen at its rising, until it stopped over the place where the child was.

Reading carefully, we notice that when the magi leave Herod and Jerusalem, to resume their journey, they catch sight again of the star that had inspired their search. The implication is that they hadn't been able to see it when they were in the presence of Herod. Maybe it could not be discerned from inside the city. In our day, bright lights obscure our sight of the stars. It's when we move into the wilderness that we can see the lights of the night sky.[20] Or, perhaps more likely, Herod's evil machinations have obscured the symbol of hope. Once away from the lights of Jerusalem and the darkness of Herod, the star moves "ahead of them" once again. It's often the case with us that we lose sight of a guiding idea, only to catch sight of it again after we make it past certain obstacles and look for it once more.

For the magi, the return of the star was a happy occasion:

> When they saw that the star had stopped, they were overwhelmed with joy. On entering the house, they saw the child with Mary his mother; and they knelt down and paid him homage.

This most unrealistic aspect of the star story is a turning point for the magi. Even if we credit the idea that a star caught the magi's attention, it is impossible to follow one, as they seem to do on countless Christmas cards. But let's not get waylaid by facts here. For the sake of argument, imagine that the magi find the infant not magically by the light of the star, but perhaps more like the process of diligent searching that Herod had in mind. But unlike Herod's, the motives of the magi are pure. The king said he wanted to know the child's location in order to honor him—with no intention of doing so. But for these wise men, finding what they have been seeking makes them joyful. It renews their confidence in their reading of the sign.[21] Matthew underscores their vision: they see the star, they see Jesus. And they are able to respond, to bow before the child. Because they see, we see and we may respond. Maybe the magi are not so foolish after all?

This is the third time the word *homage* appears in the story. It's one we don't use much anymore. In the Bible, homage is a physical act of worship—falling down on one's knees or prostrating oneself as an outward sign of an inner attitude of reverence. It is, in itself, an act of humility, one that many people resist in the modern world. A Buddhist speaker once shocked my world religions class by remarking offhandedly that she was working toward a goal of one thousand prostrations. My students cringed at the prospect of "bowing down" to anyone or anything, let alone doing so a thousand times. But even in our day and age, people of faith *do* bow or prostrate themselves as a physical reminder of their relationship with the divine. The magi, already proving themselves the humble sort, did not balk at what seemed a natural response to a king whose birth was foretold by the heavens.

> Then, opening their treasure chests, they offered him gifts of gold, frankincense, and myrrh.

The fact that the magi bring three gifts may account for us imagining that they were a trio. Regardless, the meaning of the gifts may be more important than their number. In biblical times, gold, frankincense,

and myrrh are among gifts often presented to royalty. So they are
in keeping with the magi's motives. Some readers suggest the gifts
foreshadow the meaning of Jesus' life. In their thinking, the gold
represents the value of his teachings, frankincense symbolizes his
connection to the divine, and myrrh, the suffering he will endure.[22]
We've already seen that Matthew has used foreshadowing before in
this story. He could be doing it again.

It's also important that the magi's gift-giving is not reciprocal.
Homage rarely is. "By the payment of tribute, the magi say implic-
itly, 'You are a king; we are servants,'" Powell writes.[23] From the
standpoint of the magi themselves—who, as far as we are told,
will not know the adult Jesus, won't hear him speak, won't see
his actions, won't mourn his death or, perhaps, won't even hear
of the resurrection—these gifts are simply the offerings they deem
appropriate to a king.[24] Here, they offer them to an infant, whose
power, which is not apparent at the moment, is proclaimed by the
star and the prophecy they've seen in it. They are betting on their
interpretation of the sign, willing to stake time and a portion of their
wealth on their belief that this "born king of the Jews" may not be
their own sovereign, but is one worth their reverence. As readers, we
have no idea whether this was an ordinary action of these strangers
when they encountered royalty, or one that, in a mysterious way,
signals a change within the magi themselves. Their outer behavior
offers one possible clue as their story ends:

> And having been warned in a dream not to return to Herod,
> they left for their own country by another road.

Even after their encounter with the newborn king, these men are
still magi, accustomed to receiving messages in ways that you and
I would find mysterious. A dream warns them to avoid Herod on
their way home. Trusting in their dream, and perhaps in their own
experience of Herod, they continue their journey "by another road."
They don't radically change their lives. They don't forget their families, put aside their professions, take up residence in Bethlehem,
and wait for Jesus to grow up and, perhaps, follow his lead.[25] They

head home, but they defy Herod. They choose a different route that does not take them through Jerusalem. In at least one, outer respect, their lives have been changed by this experience. The road they travel is a different one.[26]

So what *do* the magi teach us in this story that we so often take for granted? These strangers act with integrity, recognizing that there may be limits to their knowledge or experience. They take risks— physical ones that involve long-distance travel, political ones by posing honest questions to those in power. They listen carefully to other points of view and are not afraid to make critical decisions about whether or not to accept them. They are humble men who value knowledge, their own or that of an alien scripture, and their own best judgment as they weigh Herod's advice. They remain intent on their goals and, by staying true to their course, rediscover the sign that inspired them in the first place. They pay homage, expecting nothing in return. They also pay careful attention to signs, circum- stances, and visions. They see the star, they see Herod, they see the star again, see the infant Jesus, see that Herod's plan is evil. They allow their actions to be shaped by what they observe, so much so that they are willing to defy a king and take a different route home. Their commitment is to their vision—to knowledge—not power.

The magi are outsiders in the court of Herod, in the city of Jeru- salem, in the land of Judea.[27] But within this story, the outsiders are better role models than the insiders. They are better than the king, who was appointed by the Jews' oppressors and who is ignorant of his people's prophetic tradition, a ruler who fears a rival of stronger standing.[28] They are better than the chief priests and scribes, who know the prophecy and are not watching out for its fulfillment, even when they encounter outsiders who are responding to the prophetic call. The magi are better than the people who fill Jerusalem with fear and unrest at the hour of Jesus' birth and, later, will do the same as he faces his trial and death.

The magi are not insiders. To discover Jesus' birthplace is work for them, Brown observes. The magi must leave home, travel far, learn from Jewish Scripture, and search for Jesus. "Jews who have the Scripture and can plainly see what the prophets have said are not willing to worship the newborn king," Brown writes.[29] Once the magi find the child, their gifts are more than gold, frankincense, and myrrh. They are humility, integrity, honesty, open minds, critical thinking, a willingness to take risks, to act and to do so in service to others. They are the examples worth following in this particular Christmas story.

When we find ourselves on a mission, when we need direction, when we have the chance to talk to strangers, we need to be humble, honest, and open-minded. We need to share our information and ask our questions if we care about our goal. If the people in authority whom we consult are strange to us, we should still listen to what they have to say and examine their evidence before we resume our journey. If, after we have had a respectful exchange, we need to follow our own wisdom or instincts; then there is no shame in that. But to imagine that strangers have nothing to offer us is as shallow and selfish as the actions of Herod in this story. And our mission, however we imagine it, should be in the service of others, if we are to consider it worthy. If we are able to fulfill it, it may be appropriate that we walk away, without demanding credit or accolades, as the magi returned to their homes. In Matthew's Christmas story, the magi are outsiders. They see what insiders cannot see. They see Jesus, and so much more. They can be our teachers. They are strangers bearing sacred gifts.

Reflection Questions

1. Do I act on what I know, taking risks if necessary, or am I sometimes afraid to act? Why?
2. Am I willing to admit, publicly, that there are gaps in my knowledge?
3. Am I willing to ask questions of those in power?
4. Do I listen as others respond to my questions?
5. Am I willing to answer their questions truthfully, without holding anything back?
6. Do I keep my eyes open for signs, circumstances, and visions?

2

Hagar,
Slave and Symbol
Genesis 16; 21:1-21

Leaving the magi on their trek through the Christian Scripture, let us turn now to one of the first outsiders in the Hebrew Bible, Hagar. If you don't know her name, you're not alone. Hagar was a slave in the better known story of Abraham and Sarah. They were the couple whose son, Isaac, began the long line of the Hebrew people, chosen by God, according to Scripture. Abraham and Sarah live long adventurous lives within the book of Genesis. It's easy to read right over Hagar. But if we do, we are missing important truths about the salvation history we often take for granted and just who our brothers and sisters really are.

I was a child in Sunday school when I heard the story of Abram and Sarai, whom God later renames Abraham and Sarah. I remember thinking that I, as a Christian, was part of their story—one of their countless descendants. We would be, the Bible says, as numerous as the stars in the sky, as the grains of sand in the desert. My own earthly family was small. So it was thrilling to think that I was part of that overwhelming crowd of insiders.

Later, as an adult and a mother, I read the story again. Now the character of Hagar, Sarah's maidservant, caught my eye and broke my heart. She bears the child that Sarah had hoped to conceive.

Surrogate pregnancies and subsequent lawsuits were all over the news at the time. I sympathized with Hagar, especially when she ended up alone in the wilderness with a child who is crying, dying of thirst. She could not bear to watch. Who could? Who would not be moved by the lonely forsakenness of her story? But after a few moments of compassion, I read on and, consumed by the challenges of raising my own children, I forgot her.

Then in a Hebrew Bible class in seminary, I encountered Hagar a third time. Reading more carefully, I realized she was an Egyptian, not a member of Abram's clan. She was a slave, forced to obey Sarai and sleep with her mistress's husband. When Hagar became pregnant, she fled from Sarai's abuse and *the God that I believed in sent her back for more.* Unable to absorb that, I kept reading. Later in Hagar's story, when it suited her oppressors, they banished her to the wilderness again, this time without enough food or water to keep her son alive for long. But God, who earlier had ordered her back to slavery, now intervened and spared the mother and child, decreeing that the boy, Ishmael, would have descendants of his own.

Suddenly I was drowning in the complexities of a story that I'd once considered simple. My professor, Phyllis Trible, helped me see Hagar's shift within the story from being property to being powerful. Hagar, who seems at first glance to be the lowest of the story's characters, stands atop a pedestal of "firsts."[1] She is the first person in the Hebrew Bible to name God, the first woman to be visited by an angel who promises that her child would father a nation. Trible describes Hagar as "a symbol of the oppressed": "She is the faithful maid exploited, the black woman used by the male and abused by the female of the ruling class, the surrogate mother, the resident alien without legal recourse, the other woman, the runaway youth, the religious fleeing from affliction, the pregnant young woman alone, the expelled wife, the divorced mother with child, the shopping bag lady carrying bread and water, the homeless woman, the indigent relying upon handouts from the power structures, the welfare mother, and the self-effacing female whose own identity shrinks in service to others."[2]

A careful reading of Hagar's story transformed my understanding of her character and my sense of God's plan for salvation. And I am not alone. While many readers don't know her name, Hagar has become a heroine for many women, not just a minor character in a larger story of faith. To reduce her to a plot device, even to a momentary cause for sentiment, is to ignore the truth her experience holds for so many silent strangers in my own life. As Trible says, "To neglect the theological challenge she presents is to falsify faith."[3]

Hagar's story begins in Genesis 16,[4] soon after God promises Abram that his descendants will be as countless as the stars in the sky.

> Now Sarai, Abram's wife, bore him no children. She had an Egyptian slave-girl whose name was Hagar, and Sarai said to Abram, "You see that the LORD has prevented me from bearing children; go in to my slave-girl; it may be that I shall obtain children by her." And Abram listened to the voice of Sarai.

The first few phrases introduce the main characters in this story. As is often the case, their names offer clues to their places in the greater biblical story. The Hebrew word *'abram* means "exalted father." *Sarai* is Hebrew for "the princess." The precise meaning of *Hagar* is unclear,[5] but it may be a play on words. It sounds like *haggēr*, "the outsider."[6] Within this story, Hagar *is* an outsider: She is a slave, not a free woman. She is Egyptian, not a member of Abram and Sarai's clan. And, unlike Sarai and Abram, who are committed to one God, Hagar comes from a polytheistic background, notes Rosalyn F. T. Murphy. This particular characteristic "undoubtedly set her apart from Sarai" and contributes to her standing as "other," Murphy writes.[7] Hagar's social standing is so low that neither Sarai nor Abram refer to her by name, not at this point, nor anywhere in the story. But unlike other slaves and servants in the Bible, this woman does have a name. Already she stands out.

With introductions out of the way, the narrator reveals the hinge of the story: Sarai has borne no children—despite God's prophecy that Abram's descendants would outnumber the stars in the sky. Sarai, eager to satisfy both her husband and God's promise, aims to take matters into her own hands. She urges Abram to conceive a child with her maidservant. Her solution may seem odd to us, but it was acceptable in her time. She knows she can take credit for a child born to her slave, and, in a roundabout way, God's prophecy will be realized. But as Gerhard von Rad has observed, Sarai's will be a "faint-hearted faith that cannot leave things with God and believes it necessary to help things along."[8] Many of us have been guilty of that.

Sarai does not consult with Hager or even inform her of the plan.[9] Neither does Abram. From his perspective, Hagar is three-times cursed: she is a woman, a foreigner, and a slave.[10] The narrator records no objection from Abram, who listens only "to the voice of Sarai." That may prove to be his undoing.

> So, after Abram had lived ten years in the land of Canaan, Sarai, Abram's wife, took Hagar the Egyptian, her slave-girl, and gave her to her husband Abram as a wife. He went in to Hagar, and she conceived; and when she saw that she had conceived, she looked with contempt on her mistress.

Sarai "gives" her slave to her husband "as a wife." Abram does his part, sleeping with his wife's slave. Hagar, who had no choice in the matter, conceives a child. Her attitude toward her mistress changes. "The act of conception awakened something deep in Hagar," Adam Clark notes. "Perhaps it was the loss of control of her reproductive capacities or the profound exploitation of another African woman's body, we're not told. But whatever it was, Hagar stares at Sarai with contempt."[11] Up until now, the narrator has painted Hagar as passive. Now, she has feelings. And they are not good ones: She cannot resist feeling superior to her so-far barren mistress. Clearly, this is not a story about the solidarity of women. It turns on "social and economic disparity between women," differences in "ethnic backgrounds," and "a slave-holding woman's complicity with her husband in the sexual molestation of a female slave," Renita J.

Weems writes.[12] Sarai's little trick to hasten the unfolding of God's plan has serious consequences.

But for now, the narrator says Hagar felt contempt for Sarai, a detail that reveals her defiant spirit and one that cannot escape her mistress's notice. Sarai blames Abram, whom she recasts as her coconspirator:

> Then Sarai said to Abram, "May the wrong done to me be on you! I gave my slave-girl to your embrace, and when she saw that she had conceived, she looked on me with contempt. May the LORD judge between you and me!" But Abram said to Sarai, "Your slave-girl is in your power; do to her as you please." Then Sarai dealt harshly with her, and she ran away from her.

Sarai reacts all too humanly to Hagar's contempt. She invokes an old formula, asking that the harm she's suffering be transferred to Abram—she repeats the curse twice in slightly different words: "May the wrong done to me be on you!" and "May the LORD judge between you and me!" In the midst of the two exclamations lies the cause of her anger: "I gave my slave-girl to your embrace, and when she saw that she had conceived, she looked on me with contempt." As readers, we know this is an outcome Sarai hadn't planned on. Now, she's told Abram—again, without even mentioning Hagar by name—what's happened. Whether we agree with Sarai's point of view or not,[13] we can understand her feelings of being judged by Hagar, when all she wanted to do was nudge God's plan into action.

But Abram seems careless of the child he has conceived with Hagar. He refuses Sarai's attempts to make the pregnant slave his problem, still not using her name. Instead, he challenges Sarai to take care of the situation herself. The narrator doesn't tell us what Hagar is thinking at this point in the story.[14] She is, after all, a slave. Hagar seems to be caught in Sarai's complicated plan. Scholars who have found legal precedent for Sarai's wife-swap have also noted an interesting complication: "The slave who bears the master's children may not consider herself to have the same legal standing as the wife," writes Irene Nowell in her description of the ancient Ham-murabi Code.[15] "Even so, the wife may not sell the slave." So, legally speaking, both women are in a bind. Left to her own actions, Sarai deals "harshly" with Hagar. The narrator doesn't elaborate, but then Hagar doesn't tolerate Sarai's harshness either. For the first time she *does* something in the story—other than submit to Sarai's orders. She runs away. "There were only two alternatives left to Hagar," Elsa Tamez writes: "subject herself to the humiliations inflicted on her or die in the desert. She chose the second."[16]

Desperate to get away, Hagar flees to the wilderness.

> The angel of the LORD found her by a spring of water in the wilderness, the spring on the way to Shur. And he said, "Hagar, slave-girl of Sarai, where have you come from and where are you going?" She said, "I am running away from my mistress Sarai." The angel of the LORD said to her, "Return to your mistress, and submit to her."

For the first time in this story, Hagar is called by name—by a divine messenger, who immediately reminds her of her status as Sarai's slave. He finds her near a spring of water, a safe spot in the desert wilderness.[17] She has not called on God. God finds her. And when the divine messenger calls her by name and speaks to her, she speaks for the first time in the story. She becomes a person,[18] an agent in her own story. The messenger asks Hagar two questions. His *"where have you come from"* and *"where* are you going" imply *places*. But she tells him she is running from a *person*—her mistress Sarai. Tamez says the two questions encompass Hagar's "whole life," where she has been and where she is going.[19] But as a woman in distress, Hagar can only think of her present situation.

What a shock it must have been to Hagar when the angel tells her to return to Sarai and submit to her. Hagar has followed Sarai's orders to sleep with Abram and has conceived a child. Just what Sarai had wanted. It's true that Hagar, once she's pregnant, has the very human emotion to feel superior to her barren mistress. And Sarai, perhaps, can't be blamed for treating her slave harshly. But it's still shocking to those of us who know the broader story of the Hebrew Bible to think that the God of the exodus, who frees the Israelites from oppression in Egypt, would order this Egyptian woman to return to her oppressors. Hagar is told to sacrifice her own autonomy for the sake of her child.[20] "What God wants is that she and her child should be saved," Tamez writes, "and at the moment, the only way to accomplish that is not in the desert, but by returning to the house of Abraham."[21]

But the angel has more to say:

> The angel of the LORD also said to her, "I will so greatly multiply your offspring that they cannot be counted for multitude." And the angel of the LORD said to her,
> "Now you have conceived and shall bear a son;
>   you shall call him Ishmael,
>   for the LORD has given heed to your affliction.
> He shall be a wild ass of a man,
> with his hand against everyone,
>   and everyone's hand against him;
> and he shall live at odds with all his kin."[22]

So here are four of Hagar's "firsts" and the first of her "onlys":[23] She is the first person in the Hebrew Bible, or Old Testament, to receive a divine messenger. She is the first person to receive an annunciation, an announcement that she will bear a child. She is the first woman in the story of Abram's family, our biblical ancestors, to bear a child. She is the first woman to see and hear God in the guise of a divine messenger.[24] She is the only woman in the Hebrew Bible to receive a promise of descendants. This is a breathtaking list for a biblical outsider, one that most of us have never contemplated before.

Hagar is to name her son Ishmael, which is Hebrew for "God hears." The angel is suggesting that God has heard of Hagar's predicament even though she has not called out for divine help. The prophecy that follows is far from comforting to our ears,[25] though it may have sounded more positive to a mother who has known slavery. Her son will not be passive, a man of no consequence.[26] And, perhaps to her horror, Hagar is being sent back into slavery to preserve her son's life. Whether she's fully absorbed that idea or not, she is moved now not to call *on* God but to do the one thing that neither Sarai nor Abram had ever done for her—she calls God *by name*:

> So she named the LORD who spoke to her, "You are El-roi";
> for she said, "Have I really seen God and remained alive after
> seeing him?" Therefore the well was called Beer-lahai-roi; it
> lies between Kadesh and Bered.

The name Hagar chooses for God is a phrase that reflects her own experience with the angel.[27] This is a critical moment in the story. The woman who has a name, which no one but God ever uses, gives God a name that she knows to be true. It was a daring but intimate moment that we modern readers may miss altogether. "In the ancient Near East, a great significance was placed on knowing the personal name of the god being worshipped," Murphy tells us. "It was believed that the name of the god or goddess revealed their divine character, signified their existence, and gave the worshipper access to the deity's power. . . . Hagar's naming of God elevates her to a status of inter-personal relationship with the divine."[28] Hagar calls God "El-roi," Hebrew for "God of seeing" or "God who sees."[29] Just as the magi were able to see in their story, the idea of seeing runs through this one: Sarai unveils the plan by saying to Abram, "You *see*." When Hagar "*saw*" that she was pregnant, she *looked* on Sarai with contempt. Sarai uses the same words, *saw* and *looked*, when she complains to Abram. He responds in Hebrew, which some translations render, "Do to her what is good *in your eyes*."[30] The messenger of the Lord *sees* Hagar near the spring that will be called Beer-lahai-roi, or "Well of the Living One who *sees me*." Hagar believes she *has seen* God. Such an emphasis on seeing must mean something, but Hagar's story is not over yet. There is more to see as she returns to Sarai's service.

> Hagar bore Abram a son; and Abram named his son, whom
> Hagar bore, Ishmael. Abram was eighty-six years old when
> Hagar bore him Ishmael.

The narrator does not say, but we assume, that Hagar returns to Sarai. And even though Abram names Ishmael, we know that the name itself came from God and that it had been God's desire that Hagar name her boy.[31] So Hagar's story, after a brief interlude of hope, descends again into oppression.

Time passes. Precisely thirteen years, according to Scripture. During that time, God renames Abram Abraham (Gen 17:5) and renews the covenant between them, the promise of an heir. Sarai will now be called Sarah (Gen 17:15) and it is her child—still to be conceived—who will begin Abraham's long line of descendants. Hagar comes back into the story five chapters later, after Sarah has given birth to a son named Isaac:

> The child grew, and was weaned; and Abraham made a great feast on the day that Isaac was weaned. But Sarah saw the son of Hagar the Egyptian, whom she had borne to Abraham, playing with her son Isaac. So she said to Abraham, "Cast out this slave woman with her son; for the son of this slave woman shall not inherit along with my son Isaac."

Seeing again is central to this story. Sarah doesn't use either the names Ishmael or Hagar, but she *saw* her slave's son and the threat he posed to her own.[32] Some scholars speculate that Ishmael was abusing Isaac and that Sarah was justified in her concern. Others disagree. In his commentary on Genesis, E. A. Speiser argues that "there is nothing in the text to suggest" abuse and dismisses the claim as "a motive deduced by many troubled readers in their effort to account for Sarah's anger."[33] G. W. Coats argues that a closer translation reveals what was going on: "The wordplay . . . sets out the weight of the conflict. It does not imply that Ishmael has done something amiss with Isaac. It suggests the contrary, that Sarah saw Ishmael playing the role of Isaac."[34] Whether or not the threat is real, Sarah can't bear the thought that Isaac (notice that she calls *her* son by *his* name) would have to share Abraham's legacy with her slave's son. Sarah doesn't send Hagar away herself. Perhaps by giving Hagar to Abram, he is now the slave woman's owner. At any rate, Sarah turns to her husband, demanding that he cast out Hagar.

> The matter was very distressing to Abraham on account of his son. But God said to Abraham, "Do not be distressed because of the boy and because of your slave woman; whatever Sarah says to you, do as she tells you, for it is through Isaac that offspring shall be named for you. As for the son of the slave woman, I will make a nation of him also, because he is your offspring." So Abraham rose early in the morning, and took bread and a skin of water, and gave it to Hagar, putting it on her shoulder, along with the child,[35] and sent her away. And she departed, and wandered about in the wilderness of Beer-sheba.

In his earlier encounter with Sarai, Abram didn't seem to care about his son, and he listened to the voice of Sarai. This time, Abraham does care about "his son," though the narrator doesn't name which son occupies Abraham's thoughts. And now, Abraham will listen again—this time to the voice of God, who speaks of "the boy" and "your slave woman."[36] No doubt Abraham recognizes Ishmael and Hagar in the words of God, who goes on to name Sarah and Isaac. It's the second son who will secure Abraham's line, God says, encouraging Abraham to do as Sarah asks. Ishmael will survive and father a nation of his own, God says. Though that future is still far away, the divine word is enough to convince Abraham to wake up early and pack some food and water for Hagar and her son. Abraham is a wealthy man, Scripture says, but all he can manage for the mother of his firstborn is the food and water she can carry.[37] Why not a caravan? an escort? a new home? Abraham cares for Ishmael and Hagar but not enough to assure their safe journey. It's clear that Hagar can no longer depend on Abraham or Sarah for her survival.[38]

Hagar heads into the wilderness again, this time with a child and scanty provisions that won't last very long.

> When the water in the skin was gone, she cast the child under one of the bushes. Then she went and sat down op-

posite him a good way off, about the distance of a bowshot;
for she said, "Do not let me look on the death of the child."

This time, Hagar does not make a decision to run away. This time,
she is cast out.[39] This time, there is no spring to refresh her, as there
was when she first fled into the desert.[40] The food and water Abraham
had given her doesn't last long. Believing that "the child," the one
this narrator—like Sarah—will not name, is dying, Hagar casts him
out, too. She lays him in the shade of a bush and moves off to sit
down. The woman, so long unnamed, now refuses to use her son's
name, trying to separate herself from his suffering. But seeing is still
a theme in her story. Now she doesn't want to "see" the child die.
She weeps for the boy whose name, Ishmael, means "God hears."
And God does—though the narrator says God responds to Ishmael's
voice, not to the cries of his mother:[41]

> As she sat opposite him, she lifted up her voice and wept.
> And God heard the voice of the boy; and the angel of God
> called to Hagar from heaven, and said to her, "What troubles
> you, Hagar? Do not be afraid; for God has heard the voice
> of the boy where he is. Come, lift up the boy and hold him
> fast with your hand, for I will make a great nation of him."
> Then God opened her eyes and she saw a well of water . . . ,
> and gave the boy a drink.

Again, God finds Hagar, and sends a messenger to comfort her. As
Ishmael's name implies, God hears not Hagar's cries but Ishmael's. God rescues Hagar *because* of her son, just as he will preserve
Abraham's legacy *because* of Isaac.[42] Hagar, who did not want to *see*
Ishmael die, opens her eyes and *sees* a well.[43] Water will assure her
son's life, as will God's promise. She *sees* life and is able to share it
with her son. She amasses a few more "firsts," one triumphant and
the other unsettling. She is the first slave in the Bible to be freed
and the first woman to be divorced.[44] She must set aside her fear
and sorrow to care for her son. "Hagar simply has to stop crying, in
spite of everything," Tamez writes. "She has to pick herself up, pick
up the child and teach him to struggle against the hardships of the

desert. She has to take hold of the hand of the child forcefully, that
is to say with strength, and courage. This was the role of the father
in Eastern traditions. In our story it is Hagar, the mother, who has
to struggle alone, with a strong hand, in order to come out on top,
and assure a future for her son."[45]

God does not desert Ishmael either:

> God was with the boy, and he grew up; he lived in the wil-
> derness, and became an expert with the bow. He lived in
> the wilderness of Paran; and his mother got a wife for him
> from the land of Egypt.

Now even the narrator stops calling Hagar by her name. For the
first time, she is "his mother."[46] She takes care of her son Ishmael
until another woman, one she's chosen from her own people, can
take on the task.[47]

Hagar fades from the Genesis story, but her son does not. Four
chapters later, we learn that Abraham "breathed his last" and dies
(Gen 25:8). His sons, Isaac and Ishmael, come together to bury their
father in a cave. A few lines later, the sons of Ishmael are named in
the order of their birth (Gen 25:12-18). He fathers twelve of them,
each with his own established tribe.[48] Eventually, Isaac's son Jacob
will father twelve sons, whose descendants will become the familiar
twelve tribes of Israel. Tradition holds that Ishmael is the forefather
of the Arab people.

But it is Hagar who has consumed us for the last several pages.
What do we make of her story, especially in light of her being a
foreigner, an outsider in Abraham and Sarah's family of faith? The
insiders in this story are not perfect role models: Abram/Abraham
has received a divine promise of countless descendants but rather
than trusting in God, he yields to Sarai's suggestion that he sleep
with her maid. When the plan succeeds, he doesn't care enough for
his unborn child to stop Sarai from treating Hagar harshly. When
he casts out Hagar, because his wife asks him to and God endorses
the idea, Abraham doesn't offer them transportation, an escort of
any kind, or even ample food and water to keep them alive for

long. He is spineless, uncaring, and, while he listens, seems to do so uncritically.

Sarai/Sarah, who has herself been a slave,[49] hasn't learned anything about how to treat slaves. She is so eager to see God's promise fulfilled that she takes matters into her own hands and enlists Hagar, without using her name or asking her permission, to accomplish God's will. When Sarai's plan succeeds, she is so insecure that she blames her husband for his approval and treats her slave harshly. When her own son is born, she thinks only of his (and her) welfare and refuses to allow Abraham's wealth to be shared between the boys. She insists that he cast out Hagar and Ishmael. Sarai and Abram, themselves redeemed with a change in their names, live their whole lives without acknowledging that Hagar ever had one. They overlook her, and her son, in favor of their own limited understanding of God's promise.[50]

Hagar begins as a voiceless slave who does as she's asked without even hearing her name. Later, pregnant by Abram, she refuses to live under Sarai's harsh treatment. Hagar runs away, risking death but finding deliverance in a wilderness that welcomes her with a spring. In the desert, a seemingly harsh environment that few of us would choose to live in, she finds transformation because that is where she encounters God.[51] Her transformation is different from those of Abraham and Sarah, who need new names to become new people.[52] When the messenger of God calls Hagar by name and orders her to return to Sarai, probably to ensure Ishmael's safety, Hagar finds the strength to do so. She also finds her voice and names God, recognizing the place where the divine and her own experience intersect. Later, after Abraham casts her out, she hears the divine voice again. Revived by a hidden spring, she finds the strength to care for her son as they journey through the desert to safety. We know little of their life together, but she manages to do what fathers ordinarily did in those days, find a suitable wife for her son.

Like the magi in Matthew's story, Hagar is the better example for us to follow on our journeys. When we encounter ourselves in difficult circumstances, when we are co-opted by others, are ordered to do things without our consent, see ourselves as being used, we need to find the courage to escape and, in some situations, to return to those same difficult circumstances for the sake of another. We should hope that when we need to call on God, we know the divine name from our own experience. We should beware of relying on the wrong people for what we need to survive. We should do what we can to pull ourselves together and take action to protect those who are relying on us.

And when we see strangers, acting as Hagar did, we should not be so quick to judge or condemn them. Hagar is a heroine to many women struggling to be recognized by name; to be individuals, not consequences or the means to an end; to see, hear, and name God in the midst of harsh realities; to walk into the wilderness with confidence that God will find them; to tell the truth about what they are escaping and where they hope to go; and to trust in the promise of a future even when it seems difficult and unsupported. Hagar helps us *see* that the salvation history we take for granted is not limited only to Abraham and Sarah and their "official" descendants. "The oppressed are also God's children, co-creators of history," Tamez points out. "God does not leave them to perish in the desert without leaving a trace. They must live to be part of history, and struggle to be subjects of it."[53] Hagar teaches us insiders that God saves those we consider outsiders and strangers. Our claim on God is not exclusive.

Reflection Questions

1. How do I oppress others—by not calling them by name, by assuming their help without asking, by gossiping behind their backs, by judging their circumstances, by feeling threatened by others who have less than I do?

2. If I sense that others are judging me, do I think about why they might be doing so? Am I willing to admit there may be cause, from their point of view?

3. Do I always recognize my responsibilities and act accordingly? Do I step up to mediate situations that involve me, or pass the

decisions off to others? Do I speak up on behalf of a powerless person? Do I give generously to people in need of help? Do I give more than food if the situation requires other kinds of assistance?

4. Are there times when I feel superior to others for reasons that I had no control over?

5. Am I self-aware enough to escape oppression when there is a way out?

6. Am I open to messengers from the divine? Would I do as the messenger asks, especially if the matter seems distasteful or dangerous to me?

7. How personal is my relationship to God? Would I dare to name the divine? Is God real enough to me that I could? What might I name God?

3

Rahab,
Courage Caught in the Middle
Joshua 2:1-24; 6:17-25

Hagar stands atop a pinnacle of "firsts," and so does Rahab. A foreigner and, perhaps, a prostitute, she shelters Israelite spies and saves her family during the fall of Jericho. She is the first Canaanite woman[1] that the Israelites meet as they begin their conquest of the Promised Land. Many readers consider her the first convert to the Israelite religion.[2] Within the book of Joshua, where her story is told, she is the first person to recount the salvation history of Israel[3] and the first to use the Hebrew word *hesed*, often invoked to describe God's care for the Israelites, in her own covenant with Israel.[4] Hers is an espionage story with a twist: She outmaneuvers a pair of Israelite spies and her own Canaanite king. In the process, she shows us what it's like to be caught between rival authorities and still manage to protect those closest to us.

First, a little history. Many of us remember the Bible story of Joseph and his coat of many colors.[5] Joseph was sold into slavery by his brothers, imprisoned in Egypt, freed, and eventually rose to the top of Egypt's government bureaucracy. When he reconciled with his Hebrew family, his relatives moved to Egypt and settled there. Joseph's story is recounted in the biblical book of Genesis.

The next book, Exodus, opens after the death of Joseph. The Egyptians who had revered him and taken in his family, known now as the Israelites, have forgotten Joseph. This new generation enslaves the Israelites, who languish for years until God hears their cries and sends Moses to lead them to freedom. This is the story of the exodus, recounted in the second, third, fourth, and fifth books of the Bible: Exodus, Leviticus, Numbers, and Deuteronomy. Before the story of the exodus ends, the Israelites will wander in the wilderness for forty years—the lifetime of a generation—to purify themselves after some early mistakes. Eventually, they find themselves in a region called Moab. From high ground there, they could see over the Jordan River into Canaan, a fruitful land that God, speaking through Moses, had promised them as a new home. But along the way, Moses had wrestled with his own doubts. So God declares that Moses will not live to enter Canaan himself. Before he dies, Moses chooses Joshua, the son of a man named Nun, to lead the Israelites. The sixth book of the Hebrew Bible is named for Joshua; the story of Rahab begins in its second chapter:

> Then Joshua son of Nun sent two men secretly from Shittim as spies, saying, "Go, view the land, especially Jericho." So they went, and entered the house of a prostitute whose name was Rahab, and spent the night there.

Joshua, who has a reputation for wisdom,[6] is cautious. Although God has promised him (in the first chapter of the book named for him) that Joshua and his people will conquer Canaan, the Israelite leader seems to suspect that the inhabitants of that land might not yield so willingly.[7] Camped in a place called Shittim,[8] Joshua sends two men ahead to scope out the walled city of Jericho, one of the Israelites' first targets.

The narrator says the two spies—notice they are not named in the biblical text—head straight to "the house of a prostitute" who is named Rahab. Scholars are divided on whether Rahab actually was a harlot. Those who believe she was note the sexual innuendo of the language used here: Her name may be a play on the Hebrew word for "broad," meaning "wide" or "wide open."[9] The men who visit her *enter her* house, *come out* of it, and *spend the night.*[10] If she was both a foreigner and a prostitute, the spies would have been in luck, Phyllis Bird writes. "It is only because she is an outcast that the men of Israel have access to her (an 'honorable' woman would not meet alone with strange men)."[11] But we must beware of judging Rahab. If she was a prostitute, she may have been driven to it by family debts, as women sometimes were in her day.[12]

Then again, she may not have been a harlot at all. Some early readers of Scripture—Josephus and some rabbis—thought Rahab was an innkeeper. Modern readers are sometimes even more precise: she may have been an unmarried businesswoman who rented rooms to visitors.[13] But whether she was a prostitute or a simple landlord, she is definitely an outsider. She is not an Israelite, and Israelites generally distrusted foreign women for fear that "their religious beliefs pollute the pure waters of Yahwistic faith," as T. J. Wray puts it.[14] At the same time, Rahab is also an insider, a resident of a city that the Israelites hope to conquer.[15]

In comparison, we're told little about the two men sent as spies. In Hebrew, the text says they headed straight to Rahab's house, where they "lay." Douglas A. Knight and Amy-Jill Levine play with the pun, suggesting the spies went to Rahab's house "to get the lay of the land."[16] The narrator doesn't record the spies interviewing other Jericho residents or observing city life at all.[17] It may be that, finally out of the wilderness, the spies put their mission on hold because they want to have sex. They went where they were sure they could get it without compromising an Israelite woman. Danna Nolan Fewell and David M. Gunn speculate that Rahab the Canaanite was the perfect person for them to visit. "It would not be as if they were defiling an Israelite woman or doing anything that would corrupt their own community," they write. "This woman was Other. A foreigner . . . Who would ever know? The only witness, the woman herself, would be dead along with all the rest of the citizens of Jericho."[18] Or it may have been, as some scholars have suggested, that the men figured that the best place to overhear information would be a brothel.[19] While we can't be sure of the spies' motivations, F. Scott Spencer says the pair "seem more interested in recreation than reconnaissance, indulgence than intelligence."[20]

At any rate, the story goes on:

> The king of Jericho was told, "Some Israelites have come here tonight to search out the land." Then the king of Jericho sent orders to Rahab, "Bring out the men who have come to you, who entered your house, for they have come only to search out the whole land."

Somehow the king has learned not only what the spies have been sent to do but also where they have wound up. He orders Rahab to produce the men, repeating the innuendo that the spies have "entered" her house. The narrator gives a clue of Rahab's involvement before she responds to her king:

> But the woman took the two men and hid them. Then she said, "True, the men came to me, but I did not know where they came from. And when it was time to close the gate at dark, the men went out. Where the men went I do not know. Pursue them quickly, for you can overtake them."

Rahab admits that she has seen the men. We're not sure she's continuing to tell the truth when she says she didn't know where they came from. We know she's lying when she tells the king's men that the spies left her house *before* the city gates were closed at dark. The narrator has told us she hid them. Rahab urges the king's men to chase the spies and assures him that the men will be caught. Now the narrator fills us in on what Rahab has done:

> She had, however, brought them up to the roof and hidden them with the stalks of flax that she had lain out on the roof. So the men pursued them on the way to the Jordan as far as the fords. As soon as the pursuers had gone out, the gate was shut.

Rahab has hidden the men on her roof and sent the king's men on a fruitless search. And she's waited until the guards are *locked out* of the city *and* the spies are *locked in*[21] before she speaks to Joshua's men:

> Before they went to sleep, she came up to them on the roof and said to the men: "I know that the LORD has given you the land, and that dread of you has fallen on us, and that all the inhabitants of the land melt in fear before you."

The woman who refused to confess to the king's messengers that the spies they sought were still in her house now makes a different kind of confession to Joshua's men. She begins by telling them what she *knows*,[22] using the same language used in other biblical statements of faith: The land she lives in has already been given to the Israelites by "the Lord." Here she uses the holy name of God, YHWH, sometimes rendered in modern translations as "Yahweh." It is the Israelites' name for God, and Rahab, a foreigner, is the only person in this story to use it.[23] An outsider uses God's name when the insiders don't. And when she uses it, she speaks on behalf of her fellow Canaanites, who are "melting" in fear:

> "For we have heard how the LORD dried up the water of the Red Sea before you when you came out of Egypt, and what you did to the two kings of the Amorites that were beyond the Jordan, to Sihon and Og, whom you utterly destroyed. As soon as we heard it, our hearts melted, and there was no courage left in any of us because of you."

Rahab says she and her fellow Canaanites have heard the stories of the exodus and of the Israelites' defeat of two Amorite kings. The inner courage of her and her people has dissolved in fear. Is she telling the truth, or just trying to flatter the Israelite spies? At this point, we can't be sure. But now her confession expands beyond hearsay. It becomes the foundation for an agreement, a covenant, that she wants to make with the spies:

> "The LORD your God is indeed God in heaven above and on earth below. Now then, since I have dealt kindly with you,

> swear to me by the Lᴏʀᴅ that you in turn will deal kindly
> with my family. Give me a sign of good faith that you will
> spare my father and mother, my brothers and sisters, and
> all who belong to them, and deliver our lives from death."

Scholars disagree about Rahab's sincerity. Some think she is tell-ing the truth. Frank Anthony Spina argues that Rahab's is "the best confession in the entire book of Joshua, even better than anything offered by the great leader himself, Joshua."[24] Others suggest that, as a prostitute or at least a businesswoman, she is used to telling men what they want to hear, whether it reflects her own values or not. She's probably an expert in "wheeling and dealing," writes Judette Gallares.[25] As Jerome F. D. Creach points out, the text is silent on the subject, but "Rahab does recognize Israel's God as the universal sovereign, the one who is in control of all territory and who has power to allot it to whomever he chooses."[26]

But it's the nature of the deal that Rahab tries to make that suggests she may be sincere—or at least a woman who values her family. She uses the Hebrew word *hesed.*[27] Often translated "lov-ing-kindness," *hesed* is usually used in Scripture to describe the unfailing love that God feels for human beings. Rahab uses it to propose her covenant:[28] She has shown *hesed* for the spies and asks them to show it for her kin, to spare them from the destruction that Joshua will bring on Jericho. Her informed and sober request may have come as a shock to two men more concerned with their own physical satisfaction than their mission for Joshua. Rahab's confes-sion encompasses what she knows, what she and other Canaanites have heard. It mixes history, politics, theology, and emotion.[29] Her listeners find her words hard to ignore. How do they respond?

> The men said to her, "Our life for yours! If you do not tell
> this business of ours, then we will deal kindly and faithfully
> with you when the Lᴏʀᴅ gives us the land."

They make a counteroffer: If she's quiet about "this business of ours"—"the spying or the whoring?" Spencer asks[30]—they'll show her family *hesed* and protect them during the Israelite siege. Rahab takes them at their word and then we discover that this outsider is, in a way, an insider:

> Then she let them down by a rope through the window, for her house was on the outer side of the city wall and she resided within the wall itself. She said to them, "Go toward the hill country, so that the pursuers may not come upon you. Hide yourself there three days, until the pursuers have returned; then afterward you may go your way."

Rahab, the outsider from both the Israelites' perspective and, perhaps, the viewpoint of her fellow Jericho residents, lives *within* the thick walls of the city. "She herself lives on an edge, on the threshold between Jericho and everything that lies beyond,"[31] Peter S. Hawkins writes. "She lives in the shadow of the wall," Bird observes, "on the outskirts of the city, where the refuse is dumped."[32] When the siege begins, she will be caught between the attackers and the attacked.

Apparently a window in her house is on the outside of the city wall. Rahab helps the spies climb down the wall with the aid of a rope. She tells the men to head toward the hills and lie low for three days, until the king's guards will have returned from their own doomed mission. Then the men can safely head back to Joshua.

But before they leave her, the spies have some "small print" that they attempt to add to their agreement with Rahab:

> The men said to her, "We will be released from this oath that you have made us swear to you if we invade the land and you do not tie this crimson cord in the window through which you let us down, and you do not gather into your house your father and mother, your brothers, and all your family. If any of you go out of the doors of your house into the street, they shall be responsible for their own death, and we shall be innocent; but if a hand is laid upon any who are with you in the house, we shall bear the responsibility for their death."

The spies spell out the conditions under which Rahab and her family will be saved: *if* she hangs a crimson cord from this same window and *if* her family members stay inside her house. These requirements make sense—the cord will show the invading Israelites which household to spare. The word for cord is related to a Hebrew root meaning "to be expectant," Creach notes. In other places in the Hebrew Bible, the word is translated "hope."[33] The cord symbolizes Rahab's hope for her loved ones. The fact that the cord is crimson may refer to the exodus story, when the Israelites marked their doors with blood, hoping that the angel of the Lord would pass over the household and not kill the eldest child within.[34] If Rahab and her family don't obey these instructions, the spies won't be responsible for what happens. But if she and her family do their part and any of them are harmed, the spies will be responsible. The men's next words cross the line into selfishness:

> "But if you tell this business of ours, then we shall be released from this oath that you made us swear to you."

The men want to be sure that no one learns of their visit to the brothel, or her house, or their near capture. If Rahab breathes a word, they insist, they're released from their promise. It sounds as if they don't want Joshua to hear of their conduct. It also sounds as if they hope Rahab or her family don't comply with the agreement—that they won't have to spare them after all.[35] Rahab doesn't object to their small print—even if it seems self-serving:

> She said, "According to your words, so be it." She sent them away and they departed. Then she tied the crimson cord in the window.
>
> They departed and went into the hill country and stayed there three days, until the pursuers returned. The pursuers had searched all along the way and found nothing. Then the two men came down again from the hill country. They crossed over, came to Joshua son of Nun, and told him all that had happened to them. They said to Joshua, "Truly the

L<small>ORD</small> has given all the land into our hands; moreover all the
inhabitants of the land melt in fear before us."

It's safe to assume the spies didn't tell Joshua "all that had happened
to them." When it comes to their intelligence, they simply repeat
what Rahab had told them: that the land was already theirs and its
inhabitants were melting with fear.[36]

The next chapters of the book of Joshua, chapters 3–5, deal with
the Israelites' preparation for warfare. The famous battle of Jericho,
in which the Israelites march around the city for seven days before
it falls into their hands, is recounted in chapter 6. After the siege,
Rahab's name comes up again in verse 16, as Joshua speaks to his
people:

> "Shout! For the L<small>ORD</small> has given you the city. The city and
> all that is in it shall be devoted to the L<small>ORD</small> for destruction.
> Only Rahab the prostitute and all who are with her in her
> house shall live because she hid the messengers we sent."

Joshua reminds his people that everything in the city—people, animals, and material things—is to be offered up to God. The practice,
mentioned often in descriptions of the conquest of Canaan, was
known as "the ban." Scholars are divided about whether it was ever
carried out by the Israelites or was only an after-the-fact, idealized
memory of their victories. However we understand the principle of
the ban, it is noteworthy that Joshua orders his men to spare Rahab
and her family. He is fulfilling the promise of his spies, even though
it contradicts what he believes are the instructions of God.

While the Israelites are capturing the inhabitants of Jericho,
Joshua issues orders to the two spies (repeating the suggestive
language):

> Joshua said to the two men who had spied out the land,
> "Go into the prostitute's house, and bring the woman out
> of it and all who belong to her, as you swore to her." So
> the young men who had been spies went in and brought

> Rahab out, along with her father, her mother, her brothers, and all who belonged to her—they brought all her kindred out—and set them outside the camp of Israel.

As the Israelites burn Jericho to the ground, Rahab and her family are rescued and "set aside,"[37] a biblical phrase used when the Israelites are separating what must be saved from what must be destroyed, according to the rules of the ban. The rest of Jericho's inhabitants, human and animal, are "set aside" to be destroyed. A few more words wrap up Rahab's story:

> Rahab the prostitute, with her family and all who belonged to her, Joshua spared. Her family has lived in Israel ever since. For she hid the messengers whom Joshua sent to spy out Jericho.

The last lines of the chapter remind us that because of the *hesed* that Rahab had shown Joshua's spies, she and her descendants lived on in territory that was to become the kingdom of Israel. Later, her name will turn up in Matthew's genealogy of Jesus (Matt 1:5). She'll be described as a heroine of faith in the Letter to the Hebrews (11:31) and as someone who is justified by works, not only faith, in the Letter of James (2:25). The writers of Christian Scripture saw in Rahab a true convert, a character worth remembering.[38] She is a stranger who turns out to be a survivor, a savior, and a prophet.

Even if we assume the worst—that Rahab is a prostitute and that her confession of faith is nothing more than flattery, a ploy to convince the Israelite spies that they should save her life and those of her family—she is, at the very least, a survivor.[39] If that's the case, her experience of life has taught her the power of doing what she must to secure her family. If she has been as marginalized as her house inside the wall, she has found the courage to assert her wants and needs and do what she must to assure that they are met. She is the major actor in her story. Her heroism is "of her own making," Spencer observes. "The Lord God, whose dramatic displays of power permeate the battle scenes of Joshua, takes a backseat on this occasion while Rahab drives the plot."[40] It may be that Rahab is lying to get what she wants, something we're used to in this cynical age. As compelling as her story may be, we can't be sure she's telling the truth.[41] "Faith, after all, cannot be proven," Wray writes. "The profession of faith is largely a calculated risk; it cannot be subjected to scientific analysis and we have no way of knowing for certain if we are right."[42] For Rahab, and for many of us, much of the time, faith is a gamble. Whether or not we accept her confession as genuine, Rahab is the heroine of this story, its "intelligent, spiritual, and politically savvy protagonist,"[43] as Tracy Kemp Hartman puts it.

Within the context of the Bible, within the community of faith, she is believed and revered as a pillar of faith whose actions say more than her words. "To be faithful is both to do and to endure, and the vector of a person's faith manifests itself through both,"[44] Robert Coote writes. Within the biblical context, she is a savior. Her name means "broad" or "wide," and she broadens, widens her home not just to welcome the Israelite spies, but to hide them. She broadens and widens the Israelites' salvation history[45] and ours, just as Hagar's story did. Rahab saves the spies' lives and reminds them of God's promises already made to them.[46] They will repeat her words to Joshua, passing along the reminder to their commander before he begins the siege of Jericho. She saves the lives of her family and, by her example, saves a place for others who may find their faith by taking a chance, by gambling on God's grace. "Sometimes saviors emerge among unlikely people and in unlikely places," Wray writes. "We need to be open to the saviors around us."[47] Rahab's example shows those who see themselves outside the circle of faith that they may be included within it if their actions reflect shared beliefs.

Finally, as unlikely as it may seem, Rahab, the Canaanite prostitute, becomes a prophet in the best Hebrew Bible tradition. Moses has barely faded from the scene and she emerges to remind the Israelites that God has already promised them victory and "a land flowing with milk and honey" (Exod 33:3). Her declaration of faith, which she swears by the God of Israel, is nothing short of a covenant, a Gentile version of the bargain that God struck with Abraham, Isaac, and Jacob.[48] She sees the Israelites succeeding in the conquest. As Tikva Frymer-Kensky puts it, "The first prophet after Moses to announce to Israel the paths of her history, Rahab becomes the first oracle of Israel's destiny."[49] Again, the most unlikely stranger takes on unexpected significance.

Ultimately, the notion of insiders and outsiders weaves back and forth in Rahab's story. As one woman who is an outsider both to Israel and, to some degree, to her own people, she challenges our idea that people are either one or the other.[50] Rahab, an outsider—a foreigner, an enemy, a woman, and a prostitute—knows more about God than the Israelites. Neither Joshua nor his spies seem to completely trust in God's assurance that the Promised Land is already theirs. Fewell and Gunn put it very well: "When foreigners can quote Deuteronomy with more facility than Israelites can, what does that say about the grand theological ideas of chosenness and exclusivity? When foreigners show themselves to be more courageous and dependable than Israelites, what does that say about the integrity of Israel?"[51]

The story of Rahab shows us how fluid, indeed, how frivolous, the categories of insider and outsider can be. When we encounter strangers who seem to know our Scripture and traditions better than we do, when we encounter others willing to work with us, maybe we should worry less about our own selfish actions being revealed and, instead, be open to new covenants in service to *hesed*, the loving-kindness of God invoked by Rahab, an unlikely prophet in a time of peril.

Reflection Questions

1. Can I prove that my faith is real? Why am I so quick to assume that another's faith is not?
2. When all around me are melting with fear, do I have the courage to speak up and protect those I love?
3. Do I live out the idea that faith without action is dead?

4. Am I open to admiring someone who is or has been marginalized? Can I learn from listening to such a person?

5. Do I keep my agreements as Rahab kept hers with the Israelite spies?

6. Do I add "small print" to agreements I've already struck, in hopes that I'll be let off the hook?

7. Rahab invokes the idea of *hesed,* a notion that Israelites of her day thought was their own experience of God. When an outsider invokes an idea that I think of as mine, am I open to what they are proposing?

4

Naaman,
an Enemy General
Who Surrenders His Ego
2 Kings 5:1-27

The biblical story of Naaman, tucked into the second book of Kings, has screenplay potential. It boasts a handful of interesting characters, each ripe for a backstory: A mighty general with a serious health problem. A precocious slave girl. Two enemy kings. A prophet, who refuses to take credit for a miracle and his servant who demands it. The settings suggest drama: Two royal courts, a prophet's home, rival rivers, horses and chariots. There's even room for a dramatic voice-over to illuminate the inner turmoil of key characters. Irony abounds as the plot touches on pathos, deceit, pride, and punishment. Too bad we're not working on a screenplay.

In a biblical timeline, Naaman's story falls after the conquest of Canaan, or the Promised Land, probably in the middle of the ninth century BCE,[1] long before the birth of Jesus. The Israelites were ruled by what was often an uneasy alliance—a prophet who spoke for God and a king who was supposed to fulfill God's commands. Naaman is a stranger in service to a longtime enemy of the Israelites.

A leader of men who listens to slaves and servants, Naaman is proud and expects that others will treat him with respect. In the course of his story, he's cured of a physical ailment and the darker damage inflicted by his own sense of entitlement. He moves from serving his own king to serving the God of Israel by means of a creative compromise that even Elisha the prophet does not condemn. Jesus himself mentions Naaman in the Gospel of Luke: "There were also many lepers in Israel in the time of the prophet Elisha, and none of them was cleansed except Naaman the Syrian," he says (4:27). So who is Naaman and what does his story tell us about strangers and their understanding of God?

> Naaman, commander of the army of the king of Aram, was a great man and in high favor with his master, because by him the Lord had given victory to Aram. The man, though a mighty warrior, suffered from leprosy.

Naaman is a military professional, a mighty warrior and advisor to the king of Aram, also known as Syria. In those days, the two countries were often at war. And the Israelite kingdom of Samaria was often the loser. The narrator tells us why: the God of Israel gave victory to Naaman and his Syrian troops. From the Israelites' standpoint, God was *on the other side.* A frightening thought for those who believed they were God's chosen people. On the other hand, there's no suggestion that Naaman or his king had any idea that God was backing them up.[2] But now we know that God sometimes supports the enemy. File that away for future reference.

The narrator is quick to point out that this mighty warrior Naaman does have a weakness—leprosy. Most scholars suggest this disease was not what we think of as leprosy, or Hansen's disease, but was probably some sort of skin disorder. In Naaman's case, it was not enough to exclude him from the royal court,[3] but it was a factor in his life. Apparently it bothered him so much that his wife, her slave, and his king were aware of it. They will take action on behalf of Naaman because of it. The first to act is a captive slave:

Now the Arameans on one of their raids had taken a young girl captive from the land of Israel, and she served Naaman's wife. She said to her mistress, "If only my lord were with the prophet who is in Samaria! He would cure him of his leprosy." So Naaman went in and told his lord just what the girl from the land of Israel had said. And the king of Aram said, "Go then, and I will send along a letter to the king of Israel."

Although her action sets the story in motion, the narrator does not tell us the girl's name.[4] But she proclaims the power of God in a hostile land. She is a prophet like others in the Hebrew Bible who speak for God, often to an audience who doesn't want to hear what God has to say. At this particular point in Israel's history, the leading prophet was Elisha, who took over when Elijah went to heaven in a chariot of fire.[5] The young slave girl is talking about Elisha.

What a plucky girl she is to tell her mistress that the prophet in Samaria could heal the woman's husband. What a loving wife was Naaman's partner, because she cares so much for her husband that she passes along the message to him. What an extraordinary—or even desperate—man Naaman is that he repeats the slave girl's advice to his own king. And how valuable Naaman must be to his king that the monarch agrees not to just send the suffering man to Samaria but to write a letter to a former enemy, the Israelite king. "It is certainly ironic that such an insignificant little girl could deliver words of such profound importance," writes Jean Kyoung Kim.[6] Ironic, important, and essential to this story. The possibility of a cure is passed step by step from a captive slave to her mistress to her husband and to his king, but it could have stalled out at any point. Hope endures because the people involved care about Naaman and want him to be cured: the mistress listens to her slave, the husband listens to his wife, the king listens to his general. There is a whole lot of listening going on. And still the part of the message about the prophet of Samaria is lost. Nevertheless, Naaman begins his journey:

He went, taking with him ten talents of silver, six thousand shekels of gold, and ten sets of garments. He brought the letter to the king of Israel, which read, "When this letter reaches you, know that I have sent to you my servant Naaman, that you may cure him of his leprosy."

Naaman packs lavish gifts to present to the king of Israel, whether to butter him up or reward him for the anticipated cure. The king of Aram sends along a letter introducing Naaman and asking the Israelite king for a cure. Naaman and his king seem to expect that royal channels are the way to proceed, but they catch their former enemy, the Israelite king, off guard:

When the king of Israel read the letter, he tore his clothes and said, "Am I God, to give death or life, that this man sends word to me to cure a man of his leprosy? Just look and see how he is trying to pick a quarrel with me."

Naaman makes the same mistake the magi make: he goes straight to the king. The magi wanted information; Naaman wants a cure. But Naaman (and his own king) have assumed that the power to heal resides in a royal court.[7] In this case, it does not.

The king of Israel assumes that the royal request for a cure is made to *him*, and he reacts angrily. He interprets what he sees as a foolish request to be an insult designed to spark a war. He is not God, he says, and has no power to "give death or life."[8] His reaction suggests he's forgotten about the prophet in his kingdom, Elisha, who *could* heal Naaman. The king knows less than the captured slave girl back in Aram/Syria. "He sees only the impossibility of the case; she sees the possibility," Choon-Leong Seow notes.[9] Somehow, the prophet Elisha learns of the Syrian/Aramean king's letter:

But when Elisha the man of God heard that the king of Israel had torn his clothes, he sent a message to the king, "Why have you torn your clothes? Let him come to me, that he may learn that there is a prophet in Israel." So Naaman came with his horses and chariots, and halted at the entrance of Elisha's house.

Elisha chides the king of Israel for forgetting his place, for thinking *he's* the one whose power is being sought. The prophet summons the stranger Naaman so the outsider can learn what the insider, the Israelite king, has forgotten: that there is a prophet, a man of God, in Samaria. Naaman goes, taking his entourage that is, no doubt, bearing the lavish gifts he's brought from Aram/Syria but did not bestow on the Israelite king. Naaman arrives at Elisha's door. He expects to see the prophet and plead his case in person. But that's not what happens. Although Naaman arrives as a dignified figure of state with horses and chariots, Elisha doesn't bother coming to the door. He sends a simple message instead:[10]

> Elisha sent a messenger to him, saying, "Go, wash in the Jordan seven times, and your flesh shall be restored and you shall be clean."

Now the narrator shifts and, in addition to telling us what happens, takes us inside Naaman's head. Cue the voice-over, a rare device in the Bible. Naaman's own words, the first attributed to him in this story, suggest that leprosy may be the least of his weaknesses. His temperament may pose more of a problem:[11]

> But Naaman became angry and went away, saying, "I thought that for me he would surely come out, and stand and call on the name of the LORD his God, and would wave his hand over the spot, and cure the leprosy! Are not Abana and Pharpar, the rivers of Damascus, better than all the waters of Israel? Could I not wash in them, and be clean?" He turned and went away in a rage.

This outburst of Naaman begins and ends with anger and rage, but between them we see the problem precisely. When Elisha doesn't come to meet him, Naaman is offended. As an important visitor, he feels slighted. His expectations are not met. He'd wanted to see the prophet do something about the leprosy, to wave his arm at least, not to simply direct him to the River Jordan. Naaman's annoyed. After all, aren't there mightier rivers in his homeland?[12] If sheer bathing was all that a cure required, he could have done that at home. He whirls away in anger.

> But his servants approached and said to him, "Father, if the prophet had commanded you to do something difficult, would you not have done it? How much more, when all he said to you was, 'Wash and be clean'?"

The humility that made Naaman listen to the advice of a slave girl prompts him to listen to his own servants' coaxing. Knowing this about Naaman, we begin to wonder if Elisha knows it, too. The prophet's simple instructions may be meant to poke a hole in Naaman's sense of superiority.[13] This seemingly arrogant man is someone who listened to his wife's words about a slave girl's suggestion. Naaman's servants may know that their master has what Kim calls an "obsession with greatness," but they also seem to care for his well-being.[14] They aim to calm him down and urge him to take the prophet's advice—after all, they've come so far seeking a cure. Perhaps they know that the healing power lies in the source of the ritual, not in its performance.[15] To his credit, Naaman is able to hear them over his pride.[16] He follows their advice:

> So he went down and immersed himself seven times in the Jordan, according to the word of the man of God; his flesh was restored like the flesh of a young boy, and he was clean.

The miracle here—the one Naaman traveled so far to receive and brought such riches with which to reward his healer—is simple, straightforward. And still, some say, a bit ironic: By the word of a *young girl*, the *great man's* diseased skin is transformed into that of a *young boy*.[17] Naaman's healing is not dramatic, not even direct, as it would have been if Elisha had laid his hands upon him. God works in ways we don't expect.[18] Kim observes that Naaman's going "down" to the Jordan and then immersing himself "suggest more than Naaman's physical descent. As he lowers himself into the Jordan, he is also lowering himself in obedience to the prophet of Israel."[19] Naaman's arrogance is washed away, along with his leprosy. He gathers his attendants but they don't head home. They return to Elisha to acknowledge the miraculous cure:

> Then he returned to the man of God, he and all his company; he came and stood before him and said, "Now I know that there is no God in all the earth except in Israel; please accept a present from your servant."

Naaman, offended earlier when Elisha would not stand before him, finally does stand before the prophet.[20] Now Naaman knows what the king of Israel had forgotten: that power over life and death does exist in Israel. It is the power of God, proclaimed by the prophet Elisha. Naaman's simple statement of faith, "There is no God in all the earth except in Israel," is an inner sign of his outer healing.[21] It may be conversion, not necessarily a cure, that God and Elisha wanted all along.

Grateful for his cure (and, perhaps, for his conversion), Naaman urges Elisha to accept a gift, calling himself Elisha's servant. More evidence that the arrogant man has been redeemed. The story that began with the words of his wife's slave, that was supported by Naaman's own servants, has turned the great warrior suffering from self-importance into a servant of Elisha.[22] But the prophet disappoints Naaman again:

> But he said, "As the LORD lives, whom I serve, I will accept nothing!"

Elisha sees himself as a servant of God and so refuses a reward for God's curative powers. Naaman presses his point, perhaps a remnant of his old sense of self-importance. He is not a man whose gratitude is dismissed so easily:

> He urged him to accept, but he refused. Then Naaman said, "If not, please let two mule-loads of earth be given to your

servant; for your servant will no longer offer burnt offering or sacrifice to any God except the Lord. But may the Lord pardon your servant on one count: when my master goes into the house of Rimmon . . . , when I do bow down in the house of Rimmon, may the Lord pardon your servant on this one count."

Although Elisha refuses to accept a gift, Naaman, cured and converted, asks for two things for himself. Because he now believes there is no other God in the world, he no longer wants to worship Rimmon, whom he now perceives to be the false god of his own king.[23] But Naaman is also practical and knows that he will be expected to do so in the Aramean court.[24] He asks permission to take soil from Israel back to Aram/Syria so he can worship the God of Israel in a foreign land.[25] It may be that he believes God may only be worshiped *in* Israel and hopes that doing so *on* Israelite soil will be acceptable to God.[26]

Naaman also asks Elisha for assurances that God will understand that Naaman will accompany his king to worship but that his prostrations are not for Rimmon. Naaman knows his job depends on loyalty to his king, even though Naaman is no longer loyal to Rimmon. He asks for "forgiveness in advance."[27] Elisha responds,

"Go in peace."

Elisha does not scold or lecture Naaman. The prophet of God does not demand Naaman's unqualified worship of the Lord. "There was much room for grace in Elisha's theology," Seow observes.[28] It may be that Elisha and God see into Naaman's heart and do not judge him by his outward actions.[29] But the story does not end here. A new character is introduced, a servant of another sort:

But when Naaman had gone from him a short distance, Gehazi, the servant of Elisha the man of God, thought, "My master has let that Aramean Naaman off too lightly by not accepting from him what he offered. As the Lord lives, I will run after him and get something out of him."

Greed gets the better of Elisha's servant Gehazi. He reduces Naaman to a foreigner, calling him "that Aramean Naaman," and criticizes Elisha for not accepting Naaman's offer of a gift. Gehazi uses the same oath Elisha just used, "as the LORD lives," but he does not repeat the prophet's vow to serve God. Gehazi will serve himself, by pursuing Naaman and getting "something out of him."

> So Gehazi went after Naaman. When Naaman saw someone running after him, he jumped down from the chariot to meet him and said, "Is everything all right?"

The newly converted Naaman has changed in other ways. He has become a man of compassion. A commanding officer, he jumps from his chariot himself to make sure the man chasing him has not come with bad tidings.[30] And, true to his old nature, he listens to what this servant of Elisha has to say:

> He replied, "Yes, but my master has sent me to say, 'Two members of a company of prophets have just come to me from the hill country of Ephraim; please give them a talent of silver and two changes of clothing.'"

Gehazi claims to speak on behalf of Elisha. He's concocted a story for Naaman, asking him to help out other prophets. No doubt Naaman is sympathetic to prophets after his miraculous cure. Gehazi doesn't ask for *all* the riches that Naaman had tried to give Elisha, but only for a portion. Naaman doesn't think twice before he gives Gehazi what he asks, plus a little more:

> Naaman said, "Please accept two talents." He urged him, and tied up two talents of silver in two bags, with two changes of clothing, and gave them to two of his servants, who carried them in front of Gehazi.

Naaman's generosity is greater than Gehazi's greed. Naaman gives Gehazi twice the silver he'd asked for, as well as the clothing, and two servants to carry it all before Gehazi.[31] The greedy servant now leads a procession of his own as he heads back to Elisha:

> When he came to the citadel, he took the bags from them,
> and stored them inside; he dismissed the men, and they left.

Within the text, the *house* where Elisha met Naaman has become a
citadel, with that word's implications of a fortress. Perhaps Gehazi
sees it differently now that he has cast himself as Elisha's adversary.
Gehazi doesn't want Naaman's slaves to call attention to the silver
and clothing he's received. He stashes his ill-gotten gains before he
sees Elisha. The two meet face-to-face, what Naaman had wanted
when he first sought out Elisha. But then, Elisha did not need to be
present to prescribe Naaman's treatment; they saw each other later.
Here, Gehazi meets his master:

> He went in and stood before his master; and Elisha said to
> him, "Where have you been, Gehazi?" He answered, "Your
> servant has not gone anywhere at all." But he said to him,
> "Did I not go with you in spirit when someone left his
> chariot to meet you? Is this a time to accept money and to
> accept clothing, olive orchards and vineyards, sheep and
> oxen, and male and female slaves?"

Elisha catches Gehazi in a lie. Elisha's mention of the chariot means
he has Naaman in mind when he questions Gehazi. He does not
give the servant a chance to answer before he convicts him of taking
not just silver and clothing, but an exaggerated list of other "gifts," in
what Burke O. Long calls "indignant hyperbole."[32] Elisha continues:

> "Therefore the leprosy of Naaman shall cling to you, and to
> your descendants forever." So he left his presence leprous,
> as white as snow.

Without Gehazi uttering a word, Elisha passes judgment befitting
the dishonest servant who took advantage of Naaman's generosity.
Now Gehazi, and his descendants, will live with leprosy. The story
that began with a faith-filled servant ends with a faithless servant.
The disease cured becomes a curse. The mighty warrior is changed,
inwardly and outwardly.

What does Naaman's story contribute to our study of insiders and outsiders? What gifts can we discover tucked among the silver and garments loaded in his chariots?

The story begins and ends with servants. The first slave, the captive Israelite girl, is, literally, outside of Israel but she still has faith in the prophet of God. "Although far from her homeland, her eyes of faith perceive hope for her Aramean master," Seow writes.[33] The last servant, Gehazi, is an insider—not only does he live in Israel, he is in the prophet's inner circle. But he seems to have forgotten God altogether. He deceived Naaman and Elisha and is punished for his failings. There are two kings in the story, two kinds of authority. The king of Aram/Syria, the outsider, cares for Naaman and is willing to ask a favor of a former enemy in order to see his general cured of leprosy. Contrast him with the king of Israel, the insider. He forgets who wields the real power in Israel and, rather than consulting anyone, jumps to the conclusion that the letter is a trick.[34]

But there are other servants in the story. The insider, Elisha, the prophet of God, has the power of the Lord behind him. He sees himself as serving God. The outsider, Naaman, has had the power of the Lord behind him, whether he knew it or not. He sees himself as serving the king of Aram. Although Naaman falls into arrogance and anger, he still listens to his servants, obeys Elisha, is cured and converted. He comes to think of himself as Elisha's servant. Elisha, offered earthly rewards, rejects them and expects his servants to do the same. The power to heal comes from God, not Elisha and certainly not from Gehazi. When Naaman asks forgiveness because he may seem to worship Rimmon when he knows better, Elisha sends him away in peace. He does not demand that the outsider worship as he and the other insiders do in Israel.

Naaman himself is instructive. He seems to have risen to power in his foreign land because God has helped him. We can't assume that God only helps those who ask for or acknowledge divine assistance. Naaman is a mighty man who pays attention to those around him regardless of their social status: his wife, his wife's slave, his king, his own servants, the servant chasing after him on the road.

He listens and acts. He offers gifts to those who help him and has the courage to ask for what he needs. He is so moved by his cure that he rejects the god he'd worshiped in Aram/Syria and thinks creatively about how he can worship the one, the *only*, God that he believes exists in the world. And we know that his worship will be true, even if it looks otherwise. It is a compromise in the wake of his courageous declaration of faith, but God and his prophet do not judge Naaman. He is, we have seen, a practical man.

The story of Naaman is a reminder that strangers are valued, too, by the people in their own households, by their own governments. We should not be so quick to devalue them as human beings. Their lives, like Naaman's, can restore to us lessons we thought we'd learned about the power of God, the role of prophets, the limited role of kings, the honor in declining rewards and the deceit of insisting on them, the essential power of listening to voices we would ordinarily ignore, whether they belong to slaves, strangers, or servants, and, finally, the power of becoming the latter.

Reflection Questions

1. What kind of servant am I? Faith-filled or faithless?
2. Do I serve without seeking benefit for myself?
3. What sort of authority do I practice—the kind that cares for those around me and is willing to ask former enemies for their help? Or the kind that twists a request for help into a derisive comment on myself or a threat to me?
4. Am I offended when someone whose help I seek doesn't react the way I expect? Am I willing to take his or her advice without having it delivered face-to-face? Do I suffer from a sense of entitlement?
5. Do I expect an elaborate solution from God to solve my problems? Or am I open to simple-sounding answers?
6. How do I respond when a stranger comes asking for something that he or she needs?
7. Do I sometimes compromise on my conversion? Do I ask for God's forgiveness?

5

Jesus Questions and Answers
a Samaritan Woman

John 4:1-42

Many of us come from broken families. We've grown up and lived with relationships that once were, or ought to have been, close. Sometimes, it doesn't matter who is or was at fault. And even if we've experienced a measure of healing, the scars may persist, so that our efforts to reconnect are awkward or tentative. I think about that when I read this story about Jesus and the Samaritan woman. Aside from the tale of the magi, this story may be the most familiar to Christians. We've read it or heard it preached many times, often with the same interpretation—that Jesus dared to speak to a foreign woman of dubious character at a well and convinced her to follow him and then carry news of his message back to her village. The usual lessons focus on Jesus' willingness to cross gender, cultural, and religious lines to help a sinful woman repent. Then he schools his disciples on sowing seeds and reaping a harvest. But there is so much more in this story, especially if we focus on the woman—another triple-threat stranger. She was a woman, a foreigner, and, from a Jewish point of view, a religious outsider. The heart of this particular story is the conversation Jesus has with her—his first one in the Gospel of John after his terse encounter with his mother at the wedding in Cana.[1] It's also the longest theological conversation he has with anyone in all four gospels. And he has it not with one of his disciples or even with one of his critics. He has it with an outsider. Another unnamed woman, she is confident, bold, thoughtful, and open, qualities that a first-century Jew wouldn't expect to find in a Samaritan, let alone a woman. Qualities we don't expect to find in strangers today.

Years before this story opens, and long after the battle of Jericho, the Israelite people had split into two adjacent kingdoms—Israel in the north, where the capital city was Samaria, and Judah in the south, where the capital was Jerusalem. The Assyrian king conquered the northern kingdom,[2] deported many of its inhabitants to the far reaches of his empire, and then repopulated the newly won country with people from those far reaches. It was a policy designed to prevent unrest and rebellions. The remaining Jews of the northern kingdom intermarried with the newcomers and became known as Samaritans.[3] The mixed couples were scorned by the Jews who lived in the southern kingdom. They believed Samaritans were impure and that they had distorted the religion that the two people had once shared. In time, the Jews and the Samaritans became sworn enemies.[4]

Jesus and this unnamed woman were born into that brokenness. And then, one day, they meet at a well, a famous well that had been the setting for more than one romantic encounter. When the story opens, Jesus is traveling from Judah to Galilee and, according to the gospel writer, he "had to go through Samaria." Traditionally, Jews would avoid Samaritan territory altogether, lest they meet an actual Samaritan.[5] So Jesus' chosen path in this story was a bold move, one of many in this familiar tale.

> So he came to a Samaritan city called Sychar, near the plot of ground that Jacob had given to his son Joseph. Jacob's well was there, and Jesus, tired out by his journey, was sitting by the well. It was about noon.

Jesus is tired and thirsty and, though he is in hostile territory, he finds a well-known well. This particular spot was the place where Abraham's son Isaac had met Rebekah, who would become his wife, and the place where his son, Jacob, had met his beloved Rachel. To someone from Jesus' time, this well was connected to betrothals and seems to promise a similar encounter.[6] Those of us who know Jesus' whole story anticipate a surprising twist. And one more telling detail: It's noon, perhaps the hottest part of the day. So Jesus sits down near the well.

> A Samaritan woman came to draw water, and Jesus said to her, "Give me a drink." (His disciples had gone to the city to buy food.) The Samaritan woman said to him, "How is it that you, a Jew, ask a drink of me, a woman of Samaria?" (Jews do not share things in common with Samaritans.)

Traditional readings of this story focus on the time of day when the Samaritan woman comes to the well. The reasoning goes like this: In the ancient world, where women carried water from a well to their homes, they would often go to the well twice a day—in the morning and in the late afternoon—to avoid the heat.[7] But this particular woman comes to the well at noon, and she comes alone. Something must be wrong with her, a reason that she is avoiding the other women who use this well. So, some scholars say, the ground is laid for us to consider her a woman of loose morals and her conversation with Jesus, these readers say, will prove that is true.

But others reading this text point out that there could be other reasons the woman visits the well at noon. The text is silent on the question. "Perhaps she merely ran out of the water she drew earlier and needed to draw more," Tracy Kemp Hartman writes.[8] Whatever her reason might have been, it seems silly to draw conclusions about her morality from the time of day that she visits the well. Bonnie Thurston agrees: "I should hate to have my morals impugned because I occasionally go to the grocery store late in the evening," she writes.[9] So for now, let's not judge this woman harshly because she meets Jesus at the well at noon. Let's admire her because she endures the heat of the day, not just to draw water, but to have the following lengthy and meaningful conversation.

When Jesus asks her for a drink, she is bold in her response. She recognizes him as a Jew[10] and is immediately suspicious. Why would he ask her, a Samaritan, for a drink? Parenthetical remarks keep us readers in the know: Jesus is alone because his disciples are in the village buying food and, yes, it is odd that he would ask a Samaritan for a drink. Some readers add, in their heads, "let alone a Samaritan woman." While it's true that some scholars point out that rabbinic law did not allow men to speak to women in public, others argue that the custom was not always observed every day and in every locale.[11] Whatever we make of that, Jesus is about to have the longest recorded conversation he will have in any of the gospels,[12] and he is having it with a stranger, who can't quite believe he's asked her for a drink of water.

> Jesus answered her, "If you knew the gift of God, and who it is that is saying to you, 'Give me a drink,' you would have asked him, and he would have given you living water." The woman said to him, "Sir, you have no bucket, and the well is deep. Where do you get that living water? Are you greater than our ancestor Jacob, who gave us the well, and with his sons and his flocks drank from it?"

Jesus is not offended that the woman balks at his request. And he doesn't repeat it. He answers her question, albeit with a kind of riddle. "If you knew the generosity of God, if you knew who I was, you would have asked me for living water." There was, still is, a difference between water drawn from a well and that scooped from a flowing spring, stream, or river. Both will quench your thirst, but the well water tastes flat, compared to the flowing water. But Jesus isn't talking about ordinary water. He challenges the woman to think differently, and to ask him for water that's superior to what she can pull from the well.

At first, she doesn't understand. This does not mean she is stupid or ignorant, as she's imagined in some interpretations. Her tone shifts slightly—she goes from addressing Jesus as "you . . . Jew" to the more polite "Sir"—but there is still an edge of sarcasm in her response. The well is deep and Jesus has no bucket. Conditioned by years of hostility, she can't resist a dig at him. Is he saying that he's better than their shared ancestor Jacob, who used this well and left it to his descendants? She is being sarcastic,[13] but also reminds him that family ties once bound both their peoples.

> Jesus said to her, "Everyone who drinks of this water will be thirsty again, but those who drink of the water that I will give them will never be thirsty. The water that I will give will become in them a spring of water gushing up to eternal life."

Jesus explains the difference between the physical water she can draw from the well and the spiritual, flowing water that he can provide. She seems to hear what he's saying, even though she may not yet understand what he means.

> The woman said to him, "Sir, give me this water, so that I may never be thirsty or have to keep coming here to draw water."
> Jesus said to her, "Go, call your husband, and come back."

Jesus' response is surprising. Would he just prefer to speak to a man, as some readers think, or does he have something else in mind? And if the woman is married, this is clearly not a betrothal story.

> The woman answered him, "I have no husband." Jesus said to her, "You are right in saying, 'I have no husband'; for you have had five husbands, and the one you have now is not your husband. What you have said is true!"

When Jesus tells the woman to go get her husband, she responds truthfully, if not completely. She doesn't have one—at the moment. Jesus can see beyond her simple answer and lays out her whole marital history. This is where traditional readings find evidence for the immorality of this woman. Scholars point out that Jewish law allowed no more than three marriages.[14] She has had five and now is living with a man without benefit of marriage. But other authorities point out that the realities of economic and social pressure of the day probably meant that women remarried multiple times.[15] Jewish law allowed for levirate marriage (a widow could marry her brother-in-law to further her late husband's line of descendants), for example.[16] "Perhaps she had been divorced for trivial reasons by several husbands . . . husbands could divorce their wives for minor offenses," writes Bonnie Thurston. "Remarriage was the one sure 'social security' for women at the time, and this woman may have felt it imperative to remarry precisely to preserve her reputation."[17] The text doesn't tell us the circumstances of this woman's marriage history and Jesus doesn't seem interested.[18] "Jesus did not pursue the woman's marital history, he did not judge or condemn her, call her to repentance, or tell her to go and sin no more," Hartman writes. "There is no indication that the woman was embarrassed or ashamed of her story. She did not try to dodge the question, but rather she answered Jesus matter-of-factly."[19] Instead of cowering before Jesus, she stands her ground and carries on with this ever-deepening conversation. She is beginning to have an inkling of the sort of person she is speaking with.

> The woman said to him, "Sir, I see that you are a prophet. Our ancestors worshiped on this mountain, but you say that the place where people must worship is Jerusalem."

The man she first called "a Jew" became in her view worthy of the title "Sir." Now she recognizes him as a "prophet."[20] She is growing closer to Jesus' deeper identity.

The matter she poses to him suggests she was intelligent, even educated. Readers as far back as John Chrysostom in the fourth century recognized the intelligence of her reaction: "Instead of asking him questions about her own future health or wealth, she chose to ask Jesus about the dispute between Jews and Samaritans related to worship," Craig Farmer notes.[21] In the thirteenth century, Thomas Aquinas was surprised that a woman could be wise enough to bring up such a subject. She "did not ask Christ about worldly affairs, or about the future, but about the things of God, in keeping with the advice, 'Seek first the kingdom of God,'"[22] Aquinas marveled.

Bonnie Thurston declares, "The Samaritan woman is, in fact, one of the most theologically informed persons in the Fourth Gospel. . . . She is, in short, conversant in Samaritan theology (which is not surprising since, unlike Jews, Samaritans educated religiously both male and female children)."[23] So, when she observes that Samaritans worship on Mount Gerizim, not in Jerusalem, she knows full well the conversation has shifted from thirst-quenching water to theology. She has before her a genuine religious prophet who can tell her which place of worship is the right one. She is not the befuddled wench some imagine her to be.

> Jesus said to her, "Woman, believe me, the hour is coming when you will worship the Father neither on this mountain nor in Jerusalem. You worship what you do not know; we worship what we know, for salvation is from the Jews. But the hour is coming, and is now here, when the true worshipers will worship the Father in spirit and truth, for the father seeks such as these to worship him. God is spirit, and those who worship him must worship in spirit and truth."

Jesus is not surprised at the subject she raises and he gives her a thoughtful answer. Her intelligence doesn't faze him, nor does he pretend that the two of them are on the same page. He's realistic about their differences. The heart of his answer, "God is spirit," is bracketed by the phrase "in spirit and truth." The physical place one worships is less important than the act of worship itself. The place surrounds the core belief. "It is no longer a question of worshippers seeking God, but of God seeking people who will worship him in the way God wants, 'in spirit and truth' (4:24)," Teresa Okure writes.[24] The woman, far from being discouraged or intimidated by Jesus' answer, raises another point:

> The woman said to him, "I know that [the] Messiah is coming" (who is called Christ). "When he comes, he will proclaim all things to us."

This woman has shown herself to be a "worthy student," Mary Ann Getty-Sullivan writes.[25] So far in the conversation, she has not been angry or defensive at what Jesus says, but curious, thoughtful, and eager to discover the truth. She knows about the Messiah and she expects that this long-awaited messenger "will proclaim all things." Perhaps she's thinking that Jesus might be the expected one, the Messiah. You can imagine her trying to take his measure as they talk. Then he makes a surprising revelation:

> Jesus said to her, "I am he, the one who is speaking to you."

Jesus, who elsewhere in the gospels answers the "who-are-you question" with another question, tells this woman who he is. The man she called "Jew," who became "Sir" and later "prophet," confesses to being the Messiah.[26] What a revelation Jesus has made to this woman, who so many have dismissed as ignorant, inferior, immoral, and impure! He has given her the truth of his identity. "He chose this most unlikely of candidates, this most unbelievable of persons, to reveal that he was the Messiah, the Christ, the Savior," Joyce Hollyday writes. "He did not pick the emperor or the chief priest or even one of his disciples. He chose a simple, marginal woman, who is not ever named in her own story."[27]

As if on cue, the disciples return. What they see startles them:

> Just then his disciples came. They were astonished that he was speaking with a woman, but no one said, "What do you want?" or, "Why are you speaking with her?"

The disciples are surprised that Jesus was *talking* to a woman. They'd left him tired, wanting to rest, and here he was deep in what seems like an important conversation. They do not question Jesus. "They understand, quite correctly, that he wants something and hopes to derive much from the *conversation* with the woman," Louise Schottroff writes.[28] Other readers assume that the disciples' surprise is sparked because she was a Samaritan.[29] At any rate, the arrival of the disciples interrupts what had been a rich and religious dialogue that had been thriving despite the midday heat.

> Then the woman left her water jar and went back to the city.
> She said to the people, "Come and see a man who told me
> everything I have ever done! He cannot be the Messiah, can
> he?" They left the city and were on their way to him.

The woman returns to the city, leaving behind her water jar. It may
be that she forgets her need for ordinary water after Jesus has told
her about living water.[30] John Chrysostom praised her for volun-
tarily abandoning her former occupation to spread the Good News,
something that the disciples did only after Jesus commanded them
to do so.[31]

The Samaritan woman invites those who hear her to come see
the man who knew everything about her. I sometimes think I would
shy away from extending such an invitation. But she cannot contain
her excitement. Some readers think her next question, "He cannot
be the Messiah, can he?" signals doubts on her part, as if leaving
Jesus' presence prompted her to wonder if she had somehow mis-
understood his words. But Okure notes that her question "parallels
Jesus' own method: as he roused her curiosity, so she rouses her
people's curiosity, leading them to reach their own personal decision
about him."[32] It's also interesting to note that if she had been as
immoral as some readers have claimed and if she routinely avoided
the ordinary women of her city (by going to the well in the heat of
the day), the chance that her fellow citizens would have accepted
her invitation seems very slight.[33] But the text only says that those
who heard her left the city to find Jesus at the well.

Back at the well, he and his disciples are engaged in their own
dialogue, subject to the same sort of misunderstanding that Jesus
and the woman had already worked their way through.

> Meanwhile the disciples were urging him, "Rabbi, eat some-
> thing." But he said to them, "I have food to eat that you
> do not know about." So the disciples said to one another,
> "Surely no one has brought him something to eat?" Jesus
> said to them, "My food is to do the will of him who sent
> me and to complete his work. Do you not say, 'Four months

more, then comes the harvest'? But I tell you, look around you, and see how the fields are ripe for harvesting. The reaper is already receiving wages and is gathering fruit for eternal life, so that sower and reaper may rejoice together. For here the saying holds true, 'One sows and another reaps.' I sent you to reap that for which you did not labor. Others have labored, and you have entered into their labor."

Jesus moves from ordinary food to the harvest of believers, leaving his listeners struggling with food in a literal sense. "Surely no one has brought him something to eat?" they ask. Jesus knows he's left them behind, so he reminds them of the different harvests they each have in mind: Theirs, which is four months off, and his, which is ready now. In both cases, sowers and reapers can celebrate together, he says, and the disciples are called to reap what others may have sown. In other words, there still is work to do before the celebration can start. Perhaps his conversation with the Samaritan woman has convinced him that she and others like her are ripe and ready to be gathered in. Before the narrator can tell us more, the Samaritans, roused by the woman, arrive at the well, eager to meet Jesus:

Many Samaritans from that city believed in him because of the woman's testimony, "He told me everything I have ever done." So when the Samaritans came to him, they asked him to stay with them; and he stayed there two days. And many more believed because of his word. They said to the woman, "It is no longer because of what you said that we believe, for we have heard for ourselves, and we know that this is truly the Savior of the world."

The woman's testimony sparks "many Samaritans" to seek out Jesus. And when they hear him speak, they know for themselves who he is. They believe because of their own experience of "his word." But that does not mean she was untrustworthy. It was *her* experience, *her* conversation with Jesus, *her* testimony that inspired them to go to him and ask him to stay in Samaria for two more days. Now they recognize that he is "truly the Savior of the world." Not of Judah, but of the world, a world full of strangers and outsiders. "Savior" was a title bestowed on Jesus after his resurrection—except once, this time, when it was used during his earthly ministry, Brown writes.[34] The Samaritan woman is an outsider who becomes a reliable witness and paves the way for Mary Magdalene,[35] an insider, who will be the one who shares the Good News of Jesus' resurrection to his disciples on Easter morning. All because Jesus was willing to have a meaningful conversation with someone that his culture told him was unworthy of such a discussion. The Samaritan woman becomes an evangelist, in the truest sense of the word.[36]

Stranger that she is, the Samaritan woman is confident and curious enough to sustain her side of a conversation with Jesus. She models the sort of dialogue partner we all should be: willing to talk to someone our culture considers unworthy (in her case, a Jewish man), willing to work past apparent misunderstandings (well water vs. living water), open to deeper meanings ("Sir, give me this water"), willing to share what we know and ask meaningful questions (where should we worship, as opposed to the disciples' "Surely no one has brought him something to eat?"). She is patient, not proud, focused despite her surroundings, setting aside unfinished tasks and persevering even in the heat of the day. This Samaritan woman "has her feet firmly on the ground and her wits about her, and is able to reason and reach her own conclusions in her dialogue with Jesus," Okure writes.[37] John Chrysostom noted the respect and patience she showed "a man who was not only unknown to her, but also a foreigner" and that "by listening patiently," she was able to enter fully into the theological conversation.[38] Jesus found this woman "a worthy student."[39] His questions and comments don't close her mind to the greater truth he is trying to tell her. "Far from fitting a negative stereotype of female naivete, passivity, or gullibility, this woman emerges as a model of intelligence, initiative, and critical acumen," Spencer writes. "She exemplifies a 'wise woman' seeking the truth about God, deliberately, inquisitively, and carefully."[40]

Strangers, separated by culture, religion, gender, even marital history, the Samaritan woman and Jesus talk their way to common ground. Both had experienced feeling like outsiders, but both longed for spiritual truth. The Samaritan woman is an example of someone we might immediately dismiss or discourage for cultural, moral, or religious reasons. But this same stranger may be intelligent, educated, unapologetic, curious, engaging, thoughtful and insightful, ready and willing for a conversation that is honest, open, uncompromising, and nonjudgmental. Jesus' example calls us to this kind of conversation: To be willing to initiate it with a simple request. To overlook a stranger's initial hostility and sarcasm. To persist with questions aimed at establishing understanding. To use the knowledge we may have of the stranger (as he did with his knowledge of her multiple husbands) not to embarrass or humiliate another, but to break through wariness to establish trust. To listen to the other person's questions and answer them honestly but not arrogantly. And, finally, to be ready to be interrupted and immersed almost immediately in another conversation with its own set of misunderstandings and opportunities to speak the truth. Engaging with strangers is often a messy undertaking and just when we think we've made progress, another conversation forces itself upon us. In this particular story of this particular encounter at the well, both the Samaritan woman and Jesus are examples of the thirst and the living water that should both be at our core if we claim to be Christians.

Reflection Questions

1. Am I too quick to dismiss another person because I don't think he or she is "worthy" of a serious discussion?

2. Am I willing to work through initial, and even persistent, misunderstandings so we can break through to shared truths?

3. How willing am I to engage in a theological discussion with someone from a religiously different background? Do I assume that all strangers are theologically ignorant?

4. Do I put my relationship with the person I'm speaking to before cultural norms that suggest we shouldn't be talking and against my own efforts to make myself feel important?

5. Would I listen to an evangelist if he or she came from a background much different from my own?

6

A Syrophoenician Schools the Savior of the World

Mark 7:24-30

Many of us Christians identify with Jesus as we read the gospel stories. We already know what he is trying to say. We know what he meant when he promised to make his disciples fishers of men. We know that the kingdom of God is near at hand. We know why he's talking about bread and wine, his Body and Blood. We sympathize with Jesus when his handpicked disciples are too stupid to understand him. We aren't surprised that his critics misunderstand and think they know better. Often, that's our first mistake when we read the Bible: We don't count ourselves among the ignorant or the obstinate. We don't think about why it is that *we* are so dense, why *we* don't understand what Jesus is saying, why *we* don't live our lives according to his teaching. It's much easier to remove ourselves from the situation and sit in judgment of others.

But in the story of the Syrophoenician woman, chances are we won't automatically identify with Jesus. This is a tale in which Jesus is "caught with his compassion down," as Sharon H. Ringe observes.[1] In this story, he is not a sympathetic character. He's the one who gets schooled by a stranger. A woman, a foreign woman no less, reminds him of who he is and calls him to a broader understanding of his ministry and mission. This story illustrates the humanity of Jesus and his ability to reconsider a hasty decision. The Syrophoenician woman illuminates the power of strangers to reshape our own words and imagery, not to use them against us, but to open our minds to a deeper understanding of grace. In this story, Jesus and the Syrophoenician are "outsiders to each other," Ringe writes.[2]

The Bible includes two versions of this particular story: Mark 7:24-30 and Matthew 15:21-28. Scholars agree that Mark's account is the older of the two, so, for simplicity's sake, we'll read and reflect on that particular version.[3] First, some context is important. In the chapters of Mark leading up to this story, Jesus has been on the road with his disciples. He has been proclaiming his message and healing the blind and broken. He's taught about the Sabbath and spun parables about the kingdom of heaven. He's argued with his critics[4] and tried to deal with the disciples' doubts. His fellow Jews in Nazareth, the town where he'd grown up, reject him. He hears that his cousin, John the Baptist, has been beheaded because he had been preaching about Jesus. Faced with a crowd of five thousand hungry men, along with uncounted women and children, Jesus feeds them with a few fish and a couple loaves of bread. When his disciples take to sea on a boat and a storm frightens them, Jesus walks on water, from the shore to the boat, and calms the seething waves.[5]

Jesus is, we can easily imagine, exhausted. He withdraws from the Jewish crowds and seeks the peace and quiet of a private home. Here's where our story begins:

> From there he set out and went away to the region of Tyre. He entered a house and did not want anyone to know he was there. Yet he could not escape notice, but a woman whose little daughter had an unclean spirit immediately heard about him, and she came and bowed down at his feet.

The word *unclean* is a clue here. The daughter who's suffering because of an "unclean spirit" reminds a careful reader that Jesus, in the past few days recorded in the Gospel of Mark, has tried to explain to the Pharisees, to a crowd of listeners and, finally, to his disciples that, contrary to Jewish teaching, eating with unwashed hands or consuming unclean food does *not* defile a person. It is what comes *out* of a person that defiles him or her, Jesus says. Our actions are more important than our adherence to traditions and rituals, he argues.[6] These conversations, which fly in the face of what many of his Jewish listeners had long believed, have been intense.[7] No wonder Jesus is tired. He wanders into Tyre, a region that has been, in the past, hostile territory for the Jews who lived in Galilee. It turns out that much of the food grown in Galilee was sold in the markets of the nearest city, Tyre, whose inhabitants were Gentiles. As a consequence, many of the peasants in Galilee didn't have enough to eat, while their Gentile neighbors had plenty. Before this story even opens there is "socioeconomic tension" between the two groups, Joel Marcus writes.[8] Jesus himself refers to Tyre elsewhere in the Christian Scripture as he scolds his Jewish followers because they don't accept his teaching. "For if the deeds of power done in you had been done in Tyre and Sidon, they would have repented long ago in sackcloth and ashes," he railed. "But I tell you, on the day of judgment it will be more tolerable for Tyre and Sidon than for you" (Matt 11:21-22; see Luke 10:13-14).

But now that Jesus is worn out from teaching, Tyre is probably the perfect place to retreat and renew his spirit. Ah, but there is a catch. In Mark's third chapter we learn that people from Tyre and Sidon had already been to see and hear Jesus for themselves.[9] No doubt they had been talking to each other. So despite his wish to lie low, Jesus can't "escape notice." A woman whose daughter is plagued by an unclean spirit hears about him. Somehow she gets past his host and the disciples in order to see him while he's trying to relax in a private home, where only a respectable woman would expect to come.[10] She bows down at his feet. She puts herself directly in his path, as a supplicant. It will be difficult for him to avoid her. Is she audacious or simply ardent? Who is she?

Now the woman was a Gentile, of Syrophoenician origin.

So she is not a Jew, and she comes from Syrophoenician stock—of Greek and Phoenician origins. She's a woman, a foreigner, and probably from a different religious group altogether.[11] She's three times a stranger. Add to that the possibility that she was from a different social or economic class than Jesus, and she's four kinds of strange, as far as Jesus is concerned.[12] There is no mention of her husband, the anchor for most mothers of that period. "She is apparently a single parent with a daughter, which in itself, was viewed as a liability (daughters needed dowries), and this one is demon-possessed," Bonnie Thurston writes.[13]

But the woman is brave enough to come to Jesus on her own because she loves her daughter so deeply. "She bore the frustrating loneliness of being the mother of a child whose disease was seen by all around her as the consequence of sin," F. Scott Spencer notes.[14] She hopes that Jesus can drive the unclean spirit from her daughter. She offers no preamble for herself or on behalf of her child. She is honest and direct as she speaks from love.

She begged him to cast the demon out of her daughter.

This is the sort of request asked of and granted by Jesus throughout his ministry and even within this particular gospel. It doesn't surprise us at all. We expect him to agree, perhaps with a line or two about faith or forgiveness. But his response, when it comes, is surprising. And more than a little damning to our ears:

He said to her, "Let the children be fed first, for it is not fair
to take the children's food and throw it to the dogs."

What? Did Jesus just call this poor woman a dog? When this story is told in the Gospel of Matthew, Jesus' answer is longer. First he tells the woman that he was "sent only to the lost sheep of the house of Israel." Not to foreigners like you, he seems to imply. When she asks a second time for his help, he says, "It is not fair to take the children's food and throw it to the dogs" (Matt 15:24-26). So, Jesus does not answer the woman directly in either version of this story. Instead, he replies with what we hope is an allegorical riddle. The bottom line is he *does* equate her with a dog. This is, as some scholars observe, the "centerpiece"[15] of this tale, and it's sparked some controversy. Jews in Jesus' day generally considered dogs to be "unclean" animals.[16] "The Jews were not pet-lovers," Frances Dufton writes. "To them dogs were the dirty, unpleasant and savage animals which roamed the streets in packs, scavenging for food."[17] Some scholars argue that Jesus' choice of words reflected his perception of this woman and her socioeconomic and ethnic class—that she was a scavenger, seeking what was left over after he preached to the Jews. He may have been making a socioeconomic-ethnic judgment. "The response attributed to Jesus, then, rejects her request as an inappropriate one to make in light of the disproportionate share of the region's resources her people had been exploiting," Ringe writes.[18]

Other readers argue that Jesus meant to imply that the woman was a little dog, a "puppy," and that he was being playful with her. But that explanation doesn't ring true. "While some have tried to soften Jesus' retort comparing the woman to a dog as an endearing 'half-humorous' quip delivered with a 'twinkle in the eye,' this is not the funny moment of the story from a feminist point of view," Spencer writes, adding, "(women are rarely amused by 'bitch' comments)."[19] And T. A. Burkill wrote, "We may safely assume that any intelligent, Hellenistic woman, addressed in such terms by a barbarian, would have immediately reacted by slapping the man's face. And, as in English, so in other languages, to call a woman 'a little bitch' is no less abusive than to call her 'a bitch' without qualification."[20] Matthew L. Skinner rejects the notion of some readers that Jesus is testing the woman, trying to assess the quality of her faith. They are the only ones in the room, Skinner notes, "and Jesus elsewhere displays no difficulty in discerning true faith or its potential in similar actions performed by others who come to him seeking help (see 2:5; 5:34)."[21]

Even if he does not intend for the woman to take his comment personally, Jesus is clearly referring to her people as less worthy, as unclean, compared to his own. He is falling into the trap he was

preaching about to his critics and disciples before he even sought
haven in this very household. He is judging a foreigner, a woman,
and, from his point of view, an unbeliever as unclean because of
who she is, not what she does. Not what she has already done. "After
all, this woman has not asked for a healing for herself but for a little
child, and Jesus has denied her request on behalf of 'God's children.'"[22] Now it's Jesus' turn to be surprised, by what she says next:

> But she answered him, "Sir, even the dogs under the table
> eat the children's crumbs."

Ha! So take that, Jesus. His comparing her to a dog has not made
the woman angry, at least outwardly.[23] Instead, she responds with
wit and patience—much as Jesus has responded to his own disciples
when they've been dense. She turns his pejorative name-calling into
a sweet domestic scene and pulls truth from it—that there is enough
food to go around.[24] "By placing dogs 'under the table,' she accepts
in a certain way Jesus' priorities," Sabine van Den Eynde writes.
"However, to feed the children, the dogs have not to be restrained
from eating the crumbs. That Jesus, like everyone else, has to make
choices is something she can accept. What she does not accept is that
her daughter is being excluded from help."[25] She embroiders Jesus'
metaphor to suggest there is enough healing to be shared between
those seated at the table and those waiting beneath it for scraps. "At
this point, she somehow appears to understand even more acutely
than Jesus does the potential and the scope of the reign of God that
he proclaims," Skinner writes.[26] Jesus responds.

> Then he said to her, "For saying that, you may go—the
> demon has left your daughter." So she went home, found
> the child lying on the bed, and the demon gone.

As he has done before, Jesus credits the woman's words—"for saying
that"—for her daughter's healing. This is the turning point in the
story. Jesus changes his mind. "He begins the scene by assuming
that the kingdom is for the Jews now and only later is it for the Gen-

tiles," David Rhoads writes. "He ends the scene with a willingness for Gentiles to benefit significantly from the kingdom even now."[27]

Likewise, the woman takes Jesus at his word. She goes home to find her child cured. It is her willingness to believe what Jesus says to her that signifies her faith, Skinner says. "He gives her what she wants, but it still will take an additional act of faith for her to realize this for sure," he writes.[28] She has to return home. That is her act of faith. There is no evidence in the text about whether the woman believed in the Jewish God[29] or became a follower of Jesus.[30] "It is possible that she continued in her own faith practice," Ranjini Wickramaratne Rebera writes.[31] And it really doesn't matter. "The focus of faith in Mark is 'trust that a request will be granted.' Such trust is embodied in action, so that the coming, the kneeling, the asking, and the persisting *are* the faith," Rhoads argues.[32] Or, as Jesus told his listeners earlier, it's what comes out of a person that defiles a person. Or redeems him or her.

This woman's brief encounter with Jesus bristles with lessons for us. In this unnamed mother, we see a woman who acts on behalf of someone in need. "In coming on behalf of her daughter, she reveals her loyalty and compassion," Rhoads observes. "And her willingness to be least on behalf of another."[33] She finds, maybe even forces, her way in to see Jesus when he was withdrawn in search of privacy. She approaches him bravely, directly and states her purpose simply. When she is rejected, when her simple request is transformed by Jesus' own metaphor into an apparently unreasonable demand (in his eyes), she does not indulge in anger (although she may be feeling it internally). She does not lash back out of outrage or offense. She does not give him a piece of her mind and storm off. She does not give into his characterization of her, give up, and slink away. Instead, she uses her own wit, intelligence, and perhaps her own experience (the Greeks liked dogs and kept them as pets, unlike the Jews of the time). She builds on Jesus' metaphor and moves the conversation forward. She argues that the healing Jesus has offered to the Jews is not a rationed commodity but is sufficient for all in need. She is not teaching Jesus anything new, and she doesn't take credit for doing so. Hers is a gentle reminder of something that he already knows, that he himself has preached about.

When Jesus changes his mind and announces that her daughter is healed, she goes home in confidence, without asking for a sign that what Jesus has promised will come to pass. She accepts him at his word, something more of us should try to do.

This woman is an extraordinary stranger in the life of Jesus, the only person who ever argued with him and won. "Even the learned scribes and Pharisees could not claim that," Hollyday observes. "She was a bearer of truth to the Son of God. She opened his eyes, broadened his perspective, changed him and his mission forever."[34]

In the next verse, Jesus leaves Tyre and heads back to the Decapolis, also a Gentile region, where he and his disciples encounter another hungry crowd. His first feeding of the masses had involved five thousand Jewish *men*.[35] "Is it accidental that Jesus' second feeding miracle, which comes soon after his transforming encounter with the Syrophoenician woman," involves four thousand *people*, Spencer wonders. "The dogs are getting much more than crumbs now from Jesus. He has learned his lesson well."[36]

The interfaith dialogue between this woman and Jesus is a model for the rest of us. Each is an outsider to the other. Jesus "came to the Gentile territory, and willingly became an outsider," Surekha Nelavala writes.[37] The woman is in her own country, but by engaging privately with Jesus, she becomes an outsider to him. They began with a difference of opinion and challenged each other in pursuit of common ground. "The outcome to the encounter was positive because both were able to place their different identities side by side and not as opposing forces," Rebera writes. "They worked towards the goal of being able to relate to each other rather than to dominate each other. They experience power with each other."[38]

The Syrophoenician woman understands something that the disciples haven't quite grasped yet:[39] that, faced with human needs, Jesus can multiply loaves and fishes. "In the Gospel of Mark, the mentioning of bread, grain, and so on, is closely connected to the Kingdom of God," van Den Eynde writes. "Providing and sharing bread (6:41; 8:6; 14:22) is intended to clarify who Jesus is. However, his disciples have understood 'nothing of the bread' as Mark 6:52 and 8:21 put it."[40] So, again, a stranger understands better than the disciples. "Here is a model for leaders about how to serve," Rhoads says. "Here is a non-disciple who understands Jesus' riddles. Here is a non-Jew who has persistent faith. Here is a Gentile 'dog' who has least esteem in the Jewish culture, but who in the eyes of God and of God's agent Jesus (and the narrator) is truly great. Here is a woman who models the values of the kingdom."[41]

Of all the stories of Jesus in the four gospels, this is the easiest one for me to identify with. I know what it's like to be so worn out that I make hasty and heartless decisions. How often I've come up with a witty response to what I think is a frivolous question, and my listener has turned it back on me. But unlike Jesus in this story, I respond to one of my own metaphors being used "against me" with irritation and anger. Here, he listens to the woman's words. He doesn't yield to anger or insist that he is right or throw her out. He changes his mind. He does what the woman asks. He gives her credit for the healing. He doesn't do so begrudgingly or make excuses for himself. He doesn't even argue that he already knew the truth contained in her argument. He acts quietly and humbly. "Having the humility and courage to learn from one's underlings, to change one's mind, to correct one's errant conduct, is a sign of true greatness," Spencer writes. "Mark's Jesus will later teach his disciples, 'whoever wants to be first must be . . . servant of all,' . . . He must first learn the lesson for himself under the surprising tutelage of a foreign, female visitor."[42]

Reflection Questions

1. Am I direct and honest when asking that a need be met?
2. If the answer sounds like a refusal, do I give up immediately or try to work with what the other person has said?

3. If my words change someone's mind, do I accept help humbly and confidently, without taking credit for the change or rubbing his or her nose in it?

4. Am I willing to change my mind when criticism strikes at the core of my being, my mission, my place in the world?

5. Do I give credit to the people who change my thinking or remind me of truths I hold dear?

Afterword
Our Turn

I'm often surprised by how many strangers wander through the Bible. The eight we've read about—the magi (assuming there were three of them), Hagar, Rahab, Naaman, and the Samaritan and Syrophoenician women—are just a handful of the outsiders bumping into believers through the centuries. But their stories are packed with meaning—about who constitutes a stranger, about the strengths and weaknesses of insiders and outsiders, and about the value of each to the other. First, it should be clear that "insider" and "outsider" are fluid categories. We, all of us, are neither one nor the other, period. Like Rahab and the unnamed Syrophoenician woman, we are insiders and outsiders at the same time, depending on our surroundings and with whom we are talking. We've seen that it can be challenging within the confines of a Bible story to keep track of who's an insider or outsider at any given moment. Think about how complicated it is in our lives. Yet we cling to these categories as we try to find, occupy, and defend our places in the world. It is a tall order to stop thinking of others as "other," as "strangers." But if we could begin by reminding ourselves that they are people, like us, not *just* like us, but like us, we might be open to speaking to them as we would speak to ourselves. If we could be honest with ourselves about our own failings.

When we are tempted to dismiss strangers, considering them to be unworthy or undeserving of our attention, can we consider the qualities of the people we've just read about? They may be enslaved or otherwise oppressed, single, poor, powerful, foreign, in military or domestic service, men or women, mystics or magicians or simply people from another faith tradition. They might be like the wise men who realize they don't know everything and humbly seek help if they need it. Like those magi, maybe they don't insist on converting other people.

They might be like Hagar, who endured trials and sufferings you and I can't imagine. Like her, they may have been redeemed by God's broad saving power revealed under a name she knows, one that you and I don't recognize. The strangers you and I come across may be like Rahab, people who risk everything on faith as they experience it and, perhaps, in the process of survival, they have become servants and saviors of those around them. Others we bump into may be like Naaman, struggling against and conquering their own pride to listen to the most humble person advising them. Maybe, like him, they take actions that you and I see as compromises. Maybe some strangers we meet will be like the Samaritan woman at the well, as educated and experienced as you and I may be, people who are patient and persevering despite the heat, crowds, and tension that surround them. Or they may be like the Syrophoenician woman, willing to be selfless on behalf of another, willing to risk personal rejection or humiliation. Maybe they don't allow themselves to become angry or condescending toward the people they dare to approach.

If the strangers we meet in our lives might be anything like those we've met in Scripture, what can stop us from talking to, listening to, and learning from each other? At least, one-on-one. There is a chance that we can walk away with a handful of common ground, a flash of insight about our faith, maybe a willingness to return to the conversation again one day. If we are Christians, if we take the Bible seriously, how can we persist in behaving like King Herod, Abram and Sarai, Joshua's spies, Elisha's selfish servant, Jesus' disciples at their densest, or even an exhausted and irritable Jesus? How can we spurn strangers who, if we gave them a chance, might help us understand the God we claim to believe in, the kingdom we want to live in?

We may be believers, but none of us are perfect role models. We have been known to use people to satisfy our own ends. When we feel threatened, we lash out. I don't believe that we have an exclusive claim on Jesus, God, or salvation. Sometimes we don't seem to understand what Jesus is trying to tell us. And even when we think of ourselves as his servants, we forget that there are good servants and bad servants at work in this world.

As I finished this manuscript, I asked Faiza about including our encounter in an early section. She was more than willing, and she revealed some of her own reflections since we'd shared those cups of coffee almost two years ago.

"One of the challenges Muslim societies face today is the reconciliation of life in this world and the hereafter," she wrote in an email. "Growing up in Pakistan, I experienced a kind of compartmentalization. I felt I needed to choose between being a religious person or a successful professional for whom religion might not be a priority. If I wanted to reside with God for eternity, I should only focus on the afterlife. My conversation/prayers with God would not ask for help with tonight's dinner or my presentation at work tomorrow. That's too small and frivolous to compare to eternal life."

But her experience with the women's Bible study and her own efforts "exploring the lives of the prophets" has led Faiza to a different conclusion: "The only way to salvation is *through this* world, *not* by abandoning it," she wrote. "When the path to God is through everything I do every single day, then my prayers have to be about my life in this world, as well as asking forgiveness for falling short when it comes time to judge me."

Rereading Faiza's email, I am moved again. I was not the only one thinking about faith and prayer as we left each other on that sunny but chilly autumn day.

As I write now, religious intolerance tramples on our best intentions. In the world at large, in our country, in my city, within some families, we are at war with each other, undeclared or not. And while the news around me is packed with monstrous examples of what one nation, race, movement, or self-declared state can do to another,

I began this book with a simple story—my coffee date with Faiza. I leave the larger diplomatic efforts to others, more knowledgeable and skilled than I will ever be. But I truly believe that small steps can add up. That brief encounters can change people. Changed people can change families and communities. And changed communities can change governments. In time. And I believe what Mahatma Gandhi said about being the change we want to see in the world. So here is a place to start—here, with me, with you, with us.

I have seen glimmers of change. The more I talk with strangers myself, the more I talk about these conversations and encourage others to have them. The more I observe them going on, the more open I am to their possibilities, the more hopeful I become. The theologian Miroslav Volf writes about the human practice of ex-clusion and the divine response of embrace.[1] Volf challenges us to find ways to embrace others *as they are,* as broken and struggling and different as we ourselves may be. The first step, he writes, is to open one's arms, as Jesus did on the cross. I know it can feel over-whelming, the idea of embracing a stranger. It seems to me that a first step toward the courage required of us is to share a simple conversation, maybe over a cup of coffee.

Notes

Introduction

[1] I grew up in a Presbyterian household, converted to Catholicism at age twenty-nine, and graduated from a Protestant seminary, Union Theological Seminary in New York City. I have taught religion in Catholic high schools and colleges.

[2] I follow the mainline Catholic and Protestant view that the Bible was written by human beings, it reflects many writers' experiences of God, and it includes stories that may not be historically true but contain truths all the same. I believe that responsible interpretation of Scripture requires careful reading, a well-informed sense of context, and awareness of many perspectives. Phyllis Trible, one of my seminary professors, used to say the Bible is descriptive, not prescriptive. I've tried to honor that distinction.

[3] See Bruce M. Metzger, "To the Reader," in *The Holy Bible*, New Revised Standard Version (New York: Oxford University Press, 1989), xi–xvi.

Chapter 1

[1] Many scholars think Jesus was born in Nazareth, but that's a different story.

[2] Martin O'Kane, "The Artist as Reader of the Bible: Visual Exegesis and the Adoration of the Magi," *Biblical Interpretation* 13, no. 4 (2005): 351.

[3] Raymond E. Brown, *The Birth of the Messiah: A Commentary on the Infancy Narratives in the Gospels of Matthew and Luke* (New York: Doubleday, 1993), 282.

[4] O'Kane, "The Artist as Reader of the Bible," 351–53.

[5] Some of those traditions say the relics of the magi are preserved in the Shrine of the Three Kings in the Roman Catholic cathedral in Cologne. A

medieval calendar of saints records their names, ages, and dates of deaths in AD 54: "St. Melchior on January 1st, aged 116; St. Balthasar on January 6th, aged 112; and St. Caspar on January 11th, aged 109." Brown recounts their earlier names. See *Birth of the Messiah*, 198–99.

⁶ The word *magi* "could refer to wise men who possessed mystical knowledge to practitioners of the black arts (see Acts 8:9, 11) to astrologers, or to beguiling frauds (Acts 13:6, 8)" (David E. Garland, *Reading Matthew: A Literary and Theological Commentary* [Macon, GA: Smyth & Helwys, 2001], 25).

⁷ Douglas R. A. Hare, *Matthew*, Interpretation: A Bible Commentary for Teaching and Preaching (Louisville, KY: Westminster John Knox, 1993), 13.

⁸ Mark Allan Powell, "The Magi as Wise Men: Re-examining a Basic Supposition," *New Testament Studies* 46, no. 1 (January 2000): 12.

⁹ Brown cites theories that the magi came from Parthia or Persia, Babylon, Arabia or the Syrian Desert. See Brown, *Birth of the Messiah*, 168–69.

¹⁰ Viewpoints range from W. F. Albright and C. S. Mann, who wrote, "It is nowhere said that the magi were three in number, still less that they were kings, and certainly there is no indication that they were Gentiles" (*Matthew*, The Anchor Bible [Garden City, NY: Doubleday, 1971], 12), to Brown, who concluded, "There is no reasonable doubt that Matthew presents the magi as Gentiles. We can see this from the history of the term, from its use in Daniel, from the fact that they do not know the Scriptures, and from the implication that the king of the Jews is for them the king of another people" (*Birth of the Messiah*, 181).

¹¹ "The magi therefore represent the best of pagan lore and religious perception, and they seek Jesus through the best of pagan science (Brown, *Birth*, 168)" (Garland, *Reading Matthew*, 25). Roy Kotansky agrees: "Nothing in the text identifies them with unpopular incantations or prayers, only warnings through a dream (2:12), eschatological prophecy, and of course the mysterious star itself. In the Gospel, they are figures of great respect" ("The Star of the Magi: Lore and Science in Ancient Zoroastrianism, the Greek Magical Papyri, and *St. Matthew's Gospel*," *Annali di Storia dell'Esegesi* 24, no. 2 [2007]: 383).

¹² Brown, *Birth of the Messiah*, 183.

¹³ Albright and Mann, *Matthew*, 14–15.

¹⁴ "Since Herod was an Edomite who was appointed king by the Romans (Josephus *Antiquities* 14.14.4-5, §381-89; 14.15.1 §403), he would have been understandably threatened by any inquiry about a '*born* king

of the Jews'" (Garland, *Reading Matthew*, 26). Also, Brown, *Birth of the Messiah*, 169.

[15] "Perhaps it is the case that when this psychopathic king is troubled, it is time for everyone else to be troubled as well. But later in the story, when Jesus arrives on the outskirts of Jerusalem, the city is again shaken (21:10-22). Troubled Jerusalem therefore forms a united front with Herod against Jesus, and this reaction is an ominous foreboding of what is to come" (Garland, *Reading Matthew*, 26).

[16] Many scholars see elements of the magi story repeated in Matthew's description of Jesus' ministry, suffering, and death. See Henry Wansbrough, "The Infancy Stories of the Gospels since Raymond E. Brown," *New Perspectives on the Nativity*, ed. Jeremy Corley, 11 (New York: T&T Clark, 2009); and Barbara E. Reid, *The Gospel According to Matthew*, New Collegeville Bible Commentary (Collegeville, MN: Liturgical Press, 2005), 18.

[17] Garland, *Reading Matthew*, 27; Wansbrough, "The Infancy Stories of the Gospels," 10–11; Warren Carter, "Matthew 1-2 and Roman Political Power," in *New Perspectives on the Nativity*, 77, 85–86.

[18] The text "reveals and catalogs some of the standard ways that imperial powers operate. First, there is secrecy as Herod summons the magi (Matt. 2:7). Then there is manipulation as he turns pilgrims into spies, sending the magi to find the child and report back to him. Third, there are lies as he declares he wants to 'worship' him (2:8) when in fact he wants to murder him (2:13). Then, finally, when spies and lies fail, there is murderous violence as Herod's soldiers kill 'all the male children in the region of Bethlehem two years and under' (2:16)" (Carter, "Matthew 1-2 and Roman Political Power," 84).

[19] Kotansky, "The Star of the Magi," 403.

[20] A homily by Monsignor Patrick S. Brennan on the feast of the Epiphany in January 2015 at St. Mary's Cathedral in Portland, Oregon, made this point and inspired this chapter.

[21] John Nolland, *The Gospel of Matthew: A Commentary on the Greek Text* (Grand Rapids, MI: Eerdmans, 2005), 116.

[22] Brown elaborates: "Eventually, alongside this symbolism which related the gifts to different aspects of Jesus (king, God, suffering redeemer), there developed a symbolism relating them to different aspects of Christian response: gold symbolizing virtue, incense symbolizing prayer, and myrrh, suffering" (*Birth of the Messiah*, 199).

[23] Powell, "The Magi as Wise Men," 471. Which doesn't make them foolish in my eyes.

[24] Reid, *The Gospel According to Matthew*, 18. Also, on an ironic note: "It gives you pause to consider how, for all their great wisdom, they overlooked the one gift that the child would have been genuinely pleased to have someday, and that was the gift of themselves and their love" (Frederick Buechner, *Peculiar Treasures* [New York: HarperOne, 1979], 172).

[25] Nolland, *The Gospel of Matthew*, 118.

[26] Brennan, homily, January 2015.

[27] "Just as the Magi serve as encouragement—as examples of how God's grace can summon us, no matter how 'far out' we are—so Herod is a warning, an example of what can happen to us when we despise grace, no matter how far in or up we are" (Frederick Dale Bruner, *Matthew: A Commentary*, vol. 1 [Grand Rapids, MI: Eerdmans, 1987], 60). Also, Reid, *The Gospel According to Matthew*, 17.

[28] J. Edgar Bruns, "The Magi Episode in Matthew 2," Miscellanea Biblica, *The Catholic Biblical Quarterly* 23 (1961): 53.

[29] Brown, *Birth of the Messiah*, 182.

Chapter 2

[1] Irene Nowell, *Women in the Old Testament* (Collegeville, MN: Liturgical Press, 1997), 16. More on Hagar's firsts to come.

[2] Phyllis Trible, *Texts of Terror: Literary-Feminist Readings of Biblical Narratives* (Philadelphia: Fortress Press, 1984), 28.

[3] Ibid., 29.

[4] The story is found in two parts: It begins in Genesis 16 and resumes in Genesis 21:1-21. Some scholars believe these are two versions of the same story. See, for example, Gerhard von Rad, *Genesis*, The Old Testament Library (Philadelphia: Westminster John Knox, 1972), 234–35; and John W. Waters, "Who Was Hagar?," in *Stony the Road We Trod: African American Biblical Interpretation*, ed. Cain Hope Felder, 190ff. (Minneapolis: Fortress Press, 1991). But, for our purposes, we'll read them as they seem to be presented in the Bible, as two parts of one story.

[5] See Tikva Frymer-Kensky, "Hagar," in *Women in Scripture: A Dictionary of Named and Unnamed Women in the Hebrew Bible, the Apocryphal/Deuterocanonical Books, and the New Testament*, ed. Carol Meyers, 86 (Boston: Houghton Mifflin, 2000).

[6] Tikva Frymer-Kensky, *Reading the Women of the Bible: A New Interpretation of Their Stories* (New York: Schocken Books, 2002), 225. See also Frymer-Kensky, *Women in Scripture*, 87. Rosalyn F. T. Murphy argues that "Hagar's name means 'emigration,' or 'flight,'" in "Sista-Hoods: Revealing the Meaning in Hagar's Narrative," *Black Theology* 10, no. 1 (April 2012): 81.

[7] Murphy, "Sista-Hoods," 81.

[8] von Rad, *Genesis*, 196.

[9] Tracy Kemp Hartman, *Letting the Other Speak: Proclaiming the Stories of Biblical Women* (Lanham, MD: Lexington Books, 2012), 11. See also Trible, *Texts of Terror*, 11: "For Sarai, Hagar is an instrument, not a person."

[10] Judette A. Gallares, *Images of Faith: Spirituality of Women in the Old Testament* (Maryknoll, NY: Orbis Books, 1992), 7: "In the patriarchal world of the Bible, to be a woman meant to be an inferior human being; to be a foreigner meant to have no legal rights and to be discriminated against like the widows and the orphans; and to be a slave meant to have neither freedom nor right to control one's destiny. Thus to be a woman, a foreigner, and a slave all at the same time was a triple tragedy. She was not only subject to discrimination but was also marginalized three times over." See also Joyce Hollyday, *Clothed with the Sun: Biblical Women, Social Justice, and Us* (Louisville, KY: Westminster John Knox, 1994), 6.

[11] Adam Clark, "Hagar the Egyptian: A Womanist Dialogue," *Western Journal of Black Studies* 36, no. 1 (Spring 2012): 52.

[12] Renita J. Weems, "African American Women and the Bible," in *Stony the Road We Trod*, 75–76: "Women, although they share in the experience of gender oppression, are not natural allies in the struggles against patriarchy and exploitation."

[13] Gallares in *Images of Faith* (12) wonders if the contempt is all in Sarai's head, asking, "But did Hagar really 'despise her mistress' (16:4b), or was this simply Sarai's interpretation of Hagar's attitude?" Or, I wonder perhaps if it was a projection of Sarai's own contempt for her slave.

[14] Gallares, *Images of Faith*, 12.

[15] Nowell, *Women in the Old Testament*, 14.

[16] Elsa Tamez, "The Woman Who Complicated the History of Salvation," *CrossCurrents* 36, no. 2 (Summer 1986): 133.

[17] Phyllis Trible, "Ominous Beginnings for a Promise of Blessing," in *Hagar, Sarah, and Their Children: Jewish, Christian, and Muslim Perspectives*, ed. Trible and Letty M. Russell (Louisville, KY: Westminster John Knox, 2006), 40: "The Hebrew word 'spring' (*'ayn*) also means 'eye.' The association

resonates with Hagar's having acquired a new vision of Sarai, and it antici-
pates the new vision of God that she will soon acquire."

[18] Gallares, *Images of Faith*, 15.

[19] "These are not simple rhetorical questions, they are full of meaning.
They cover her whole life" (Tamez, "The Woman Who Complicated the
History of Salvation," 136).

[20] Frymer-Kensky, *Reading the Women of the Bible*, 230–31.

[21] Tamez goes on to say that only by being born in Abram's house
and being circumcised will Ishmael receive the rights of inheritance and
be part of salvation history. Tamez, "The Woman Who Complicated the
History of Salvation," 137.

[22] These lines sometimes are quoted to justify the perception that Arabs,
the descendants of Ishmael, and Muslims, in general, are "naturally" in
conflict with the rest of the world. But, inspired by Trible, I see these words
as descriptive, not prescriptive. Some Arabs and/or Muslims, like any of
us, may be in conflict with other peoples at some times in some places,
but they are not always and they don't need to be.

[23] "Hagar is the first person to be visited by an angel. She is the first to
hear an announcement of birth. She is the first woman to bear a child in the
story of the ancestors (Gen 12–50). She is promised descendants in the same
terms that such promises are given to male ancestors (Gen 16:10; cf. Gen
15:5; 17:5-6; 22:16; 26:4; 28:14)" (Nowell, *Women in the Old Testament*, 16).

[24] The angel or messenger of this story and God are "obviously one and
the same person. The angel of the Lord is therefore a form in which Yahweh appears (*eine Erscheinungsform Jahwes*). He is God himself in human
form" (von Rad, *Genesis*, 193). See also J. Cheryl Exum, "Hagar *en Procès*:
The Abject in Search of Subjectivity," *From the Margins 1: Women of the
Hebrew Bible and their Afterlives*, ed. Peter S. Hawkins and Lesleigh Cushing
Stahlberg, 9 (Sheffield: Sheffield Phoenix Press, 2009).

[25] See Frymer-Kensky, *Women in Scripture*, 86–87.

[26] Trible, *Texts of Terror*, 17: "Suffering undercuts hope. A sword pierces
Hagar's own soul. The divine promise of Ishmael means life at the bound-
ary of consolation and desolation."

[27] Trible, "Ominous Beginnings," 41: "The narrator introduces her
words with a striking expression that accords her a power attributed to no
one else in the Bible. Hagar 'calls the name of the Lord who spoke to her'
(Gen 16:13). She does not invoke the Lord; she names the Lord. She calls

the name; she does not call *upon* the name." See also Clark, "Hagar the Egyptian," 53: "Hagar did not call upon Yahweh, the god of her slave-holders Abram and Sarai. Rather, she names and petitions God from her own tradition to deliver her from the wilderness."

[28] Murphy, "Sista-Hoods," 86–87.

[29] "God calls Hagar by name, the only character in the story to do so, and Hagar responds, naming God El Roi, 'God of my seeing,' which can mean both 'the God I have seen' and 'the God who sees me'" (Frymer-Kensky, *Reading the Women of the Bible*, 231). See also Trible, "Ominous Beginnings," 39: "Hagar's vision and Sarai's vision have brought her to this spring, itself a play on the word for 'eye.' Now the mutual 'seeing' between God and Hagar points to a solution."

[30] Danna Nolan Fewell and David M. Gunn, *Gender, Power, and Promise: The Subject of the Bible's First Story* (Nashville: Abingdon Press, 1993), 46.

[31] Trible, *Texts of Terror*, 19: Abram naming Ishmael "strips Hagar of the power that God gave her."

[32] Trible, "Ominous Beginnings," 44.

[33] E. A. Speiser, *Genesis*, The Anchor Bible (New York: Doubleday, 1962), 155. John S. Kselman translates v. 9 as "Sarah saw Hagar the Egyptian's son, whom she had borne to Abraham 'Isaacing,'" that is, "taking the place of Sarah's son Isaac," in "Genesis," *Harper's Bible Commentary*, revised ed., ed. James L. Mays, 96 (San Francisco: HarperCollins, 2000).

[34] G. W. Coats, *Genesis* (Grand Rapids, MI: Eerdmans, 1983), 153.

[35] Careful readers will note that Ishmael was probably too old for Hagar to carry him on her shoulder, but this detail is too small to derail the story.

[36] Fewell and Gunn, *Gender, Power, and Promise*, 51. See also Frymer-Kensky, *Reading the Women of the Bible*, 231.

[37] Fewell and Gunn, *Gender, Power, and Promise*, 51. See also Trible, "Ominous Beginnings," 47.

[38] Murphy, "Sista-Hoods," 88.

[39] Fewell and Gunn, *Gender, Power, and Promise*, 52.

[40] Trible, *Texts of Terror*, 25.

[41] Ibid.: "Her grief, like her speech, is sufficient unto itself. She does not cry out to another; she does not beseech God. A madonna alone with her dying child, Hagar weeps."

[42] Frymer-Kensky, *Women in Scripture*, 87: "God then saves the dying Ishmael, not because of Hagar's cries or God's promises to Abram, but

because God heard Ishmael's voice (Gen. 21:15-21). God's relationship with Hagar is resealed with her son, as God's relationship with Abram is resealed with Isaac, and his son Jacob." See also Trible, *Texts of Terror*, 26.

[43] Trible, "Ominous Beginnings," 49: "The water of weeping yields to the water of life."

[44] Ibid., 46.

[45] Tamez, "The Woman Who Complicated the History of Salvation," 138: Hagar is, therefore, a model for "many poor Latin American women who, abandoned by their husbands, watch over and doubly protect their families."

[46] Trible, "Ominous Beginnings," 50: "For the last time Hagar appears in the Hebrew Bible, and for the first time she is called 'mother.'"

[47] Ibid.: "By his mother's action Ishmael acquires the indispensable possession for a future." The fact that Hagar finds Ishmael a wife may suggest she had "financial resources." See Waters, "Who Was Hagar?," 202.

[48] Waters sees "no bitterness" in Ishmael when he meets Isaac to bury their father. See Waters, "Who Was Hagar?," 199.

[49] See Genesis 12. "Sarai's own experience as a slave does not make her more empathetic to the slave in her own home. On the contrary, it makes her want to assert her dominance and authority so she won't lose it again" (Frymer-Kensky, *Reading the Women of the Bible*, 232).

[50] Fewell and Gunn, *Gender, Power, and Promise*, 52: "God attempts to make up for human failing. As Abraham and Sarah circumscribe their divinely blessed family, God envelops Hagar and her son in blessing and promise as well."

[51] Murphy, "Sista-Hoods," 85.

[52] Ibid., 90.

[53] Tamez, "The Woman Who Complicated the History of Salvation," 136.

Chapter 3

[1] Bradley L. Crowell, "Good Girl, Bad Girl: Foreign Women of the Deuteronomistic History in Postcolonial Perspective," *Biblical Interpretation* 21, no. 1 (2013): 7.

[2] T. J. Wray, *Good Girls, Bad Girls: The Enduring Lessons of Twelve Women of the Old Testament* (Lanham, MD: Rowman & Littlefield, 2008), 48.

[3] Robert G. Boling and G. Ernest Wright, *Joshua: A New Translation with Notes and Commentary*, The Anchor Bible (Garden City, NY: Doubleday, 1982), 146.

[4] Ibid., 147.

[5] Which probably was a coat with long sleeves, not many colors. But that's a different story.

[6] Deuteronomy 34:9 says he was "full of the spirit of wisdom, because Moses had laid his hands on him."

[7] What biblical scholars call "the conquest of Canaan" may or may not have been as violent as the Bible implies. For a summary of three theories, see Tracy Kemp Hartman, *Letting the Other Speak: Proclaiming the Stories of Biblical Women* (Lanham, MD: Lexington Books, 2012), 25–26.

[8] Shittim is the place where the Israelite men have disastrous encounters with foreign women. See Numbers 25 and Danna Nolan Fewell, "Joshua," in *The Women's Bible Commentary*, ed. Carol A. Newsom and Sharon H. Ringe, 66 (Louisville, KY: Westminster John Knox, 1992).

[9] William L. Lyons, "Rahab in Rehab: Christian Interpretation of the Madame from Jericho," in *Women in the Biblical World: A Survey of Old and New Testament Perspectives*, ed. Elizabeth A. McCabe, 34 (Lanham, MD: University Press of America, 2009). See also Tikva Frymer-Kensky, *Reading the Women of the Bible: A New Interpretation of Their Stories* (New York: Schocken Books, 2002), 44: "Her name is emblematic of the permissible boundaries of Israel. She is the wide-open woman who is the wide-open door to Canaan, or maybe (in the negative view) the wide-open door to apostasy."

[10] Jerome F. D. Creach, *Joshua*, Interpretation: A Bible Commentary for Teaching and Preaching (Louisville, KY: Westminster John Knox, 1991), 32.

[11] Phyllis Bird, "The Harlot as Heroine," *Semeia* 46 (1989): 130.

[12] Robert B. Coote, *Joshua*, The New Interpreter's Bible: A Commentary in Twelve Volumes, vol. II (Nashville: Abingdon Press, 1998), 593. See also Creach, *Joshua*, 33: "Rahab was the victim of an economic system in which women had no opportunities to earn a living; women like her sometimes found themselves on the edge of life, with slavery or prostitution their only options."

[13] See Janice Nunnally-Cox, *Foremothers: Women of the Bible* (New York: Seabury Press, 1981), 44.

[14] Wray, *Good Girls, Bad Girls*, 51.

[15] Hartman, *Letting the Other Speak*, 25.

[16] Douglas A. Knight and Amy-Jill Levine, *The Meaning of the Bible: What the Jewish Scriptures and Christian Old Testament Can Teach Us* (New York: HarperCollins, 2011), 276.

[17] Boling and Wright, *Joshua*, 145.

[18] Danna Nolan Fewell and David M. Gunn, *Gender, Power, and Promise: The Subject of the Bible's First Story* (Nashville: Abingdon Press, 1993), 117–18.

[19] "The spies' behavior has been commonly defended by the argument that a brothel would be the best place for them to secure information about the city. The text, however, gives no indication that their place of lodging is, in fact, a brothel" (Fewell and Gunn, *Gender, Power, and Promise*, 117). See also Aaron Sherwood, "A Leader's Misleading and a Prostitute's Profession: A Re-examination of Joshua 2," *Journal for the Study of the Old Testament* 31, no. 1 (2006): 48. See also Boling and Wright, *Joshua*, 145; and Bird, "Harlot as Heroine," 128.

[20] F. Scott Spencer, *Dancing Girls, Loose Ladies, and Women of the Cloth: The Women in Jesus' Life* (New York: Continuum, 2004), 30.

[21] Creach, *Joshua*, 34. Now, from her perspective, the outsiders are insiders.

[22] Frymer-Kensky, *Reading the Women of the Bible*, 297–98: "She speaks in the pattern of other statements of faith, using the 'I know' with which Moses' father-in-law Jethro declared after the Exodus, 'Now I know that the Lord is greater than all gods (Exod. 18:11).'"

[23] "The spies' use in v. 14 is at Rahab's behest, and in v. 24 a report of her own words" (Sherwood, "A Leader's Misleading," 55).

[24] Hartman, *Letting the Other Speak*, 30, citing Spina (*The Faith of the Outsider: Exclusion and Inclusion in the Biblical Story* [Grand Rapids, MI: Eerdmans, 2005]): "He notes that only two other persons in Scripture, Moses and Solomon, use the phrase 'YHWH is God in the earth below.'"

[25] Judette A. Gallares, *Images of Faith: Spirituality of Women in the Old Testament* (Maryknoll, NY: Orbis Books, 1992), 41.

[26] Creach, *Joshua*, 36.

[27] Peter S. Hawkins, "God's Trophy Whore," in *From the Margins 1: Women of the Hebrew Bible and their Afterlives*, ed. Hawkins and Lesleigh Cushing Stahlberg, 54–55 (Sheffield: Sheffield Phoenix Press, 2009).

[28] Ibid., 55.

[29] Ibid., 54: "She is a mistress of rhetoric, indeed, more eloquent than many of the more estimable Hebrew women encountered in the Pentateuch."

[30] Spencer, *Dancing Girls*, 31: "Instead of spontaneously responding to Rahab with deep gratitude and commitment—they owe her their lives, after all—they mechanically impose a set of rules and regulations in a pathetic last-ditch effort to reclaim some of the dignity and authority they've forfeited throughout the story. They might even have hoped Rahab would slip up so they would no longer be indebted to a Canaanite prostitute."

[31] Hawkins, "God's Trophy Whore," 52.

[32] Bird, "Harlot as Heroine," 121.

[33] Creach, *Joshua*, 38.

[34] J. Alberto Soggin, *Joshua: A Commentary*, The Old Testament Library (Philadelphia: Westminster Press, 1970), 42. See also Hawkins, "God's Trophy Whore," 56; and Creach, *Joshua*, 37. Crowell, "Good Girl, Bad Girl," 7, points out that the cord "could have sexual implications, as a crimson cord is an image of a woman's lips elsewhere (see Cant. 4:3)."

[35] Fewell and Gunn, *Gender, Power, and Promise*, 119–20.

[36] Ibid., 120.

[37] Perhaps as a form of "cultic quarantine," lest her beliefs infect those of the Israelites. See Hawkins, "God's Trophy Whore," 57; and Creach, *Joshua*, 66.

[38] Lyons, "Rahab in Rehab," 32.

[39] Fewell and Gunn, *Gender, Power, and Promise*, 120.

[40] Spencer, *Dancing Girls*, 31.

[41] "Whether Rahab's recitation of Israel's salvation history shows her theological fidelity to the God of Israel or whether she is a realist who acts in order to preserve her family cannot be determined. As is often the case with biblical narratives, motives, especially those of women, remain suppressed" (Knight and Levine, *The Meaning of the Bible*, 276).

[42] Wray, *Good Girls, Bad Girls*, 52.

[43] Hartman, *Letting the Other Speak*, 30.

[44] Coote, *Joshua*, 596: "The figure of Rahab reminds the interpreter that faith may be expounded in terms not only of doctrine, but also of lives lived."

[45] "Because Rahab widened her house to allow the spies to enter, the kingdom of God became a wider place (i.e., including Gentiles), and

eventually her wideness was heard around the world" (Lyons, "Rahab in Rehab," 34).

⁴⁶ Frymer-Kensky, *Reading the Women of the Bible*, 35.

⁴⁷ Wray, *Good Girls, Bad Girls*, 53.

⁴⁸ See Hawkins, "God's Trophy Whore," 55.

⁴⁹ Frymer-Kensky, *Reading the Women of the Bible*, 298.

⁵⁰ See Hartman, *Letting the Other Speak*, 30.

⁵¹ Fewell and Gunn, *Gender, Power, and Promise*, 120.

Chapter 4

¹ T. R. Hobbs, "Naaman," *The Anchor Bible Dictionary*, vol. 4, ed. David Noel Freedman, 967 (New York: Doubleday, 1992).

² Burke O. Long, *2 Kings*, vol. X, The Forms of the Old Testament Literature, ed. Rolf P. Knierim and Gene M. Tucker (Grand Rapids, MI: Eerdmans, 1991), 70: "It is the God of Israel who has given victories to Aram through this afflicted hero . . . the cause of his fame is unknown to his admirers and perhaps hidden even from himself." And A. Graeme Auld, *I and II Kings*, The Daily Study Bible Series (Louisville, KY: Westminster John Knox, 1986), 167.

³ Mordechai Cogan and Hayim Tadmor, *II Kings: A New Translation with Introduction and Commentary*, The Anchor Yale Bible, vol. II (New Haven, CT: Yale University Press, 1988), 63.

⁴ Jean Kyoung Kim has reimagined the story of Naaman and amplified the role of the servant girl. See "Reading and Retelling Naaman's Story (2 Kings 5)," *Journal for the Study of the Old Testament* 30, no. 1 (2005): 49–61.

⁵ Again, that's another story. See 2 Kings 2.

⁶ Kim, "Reading and Retelling," 104.

⁷ Walter Brueggemann and Davis Hawkins, "The Affirmation of Prophetic Power and Deconstruction of Royal Authority in the Elisha Narratives," *The Catholic Biblical Quarterly* 76, no. 1 (2014): 63.

⁸ "With this rhetorical question by the king of Israel, the writer mocks the importance of royal authority" (Robert L. Cohn, *2 Kings*, Berit Olam: Studies in Hebrew Narrative & Poetry, ed. David W. Cotter, 37 [Collegeville, MN: Liturgical Press, 2000]).

⁹ Choon-Leong Seow, "2 Kings," *New Interpreter's Bible*, vol. III (Nashville: Abingdon Press, 1999), 192.

[10] Cohn, *2 Kings*, 37: "Naaman may have come like a conquering hero, 'with his horses and chariots' (v. 9), but Elisha asserts his own authority by dismissing him without an audience."

[11] Ibid.: "The writer focuses on the discomfiture of the haughty but ailing fieldmarshal by offering a rare biblical look into the thoughts of this, until now, silent character. Attention begins to shift from the cure to the mentality of the patient."

[12] Volkmar Fritz, *1 & 2 Kings: A Continental Commentary*, trans. Anselm Hagedorn (Minneapolis: Fortress Press, 2003), 259.

[13] Cohn, *2 Kings*, 37: "All at once the blank figure of Naaman is shaded in, and we suspect that Elisha's instruction, in its simplicity, is designed to cure this arrogant Aramean of more than his leprosy."

[14] "Something small is easier to perform than something great. Yet, for Naaman, the opposite is the case. The servant's request reveals Naaman's obsession with greatness" (Kim, "Reading and Retelling," 55). See also Auld, *I and II Kings*, 168: "They both know him and perhaps care for him—he had after all inspired loyalty and concern even in a captured Israelite slave girl. They have also more experience than their master of being at the receiving end of official highhandedness."

[15] Marvin A. Sweeney, *I & II Kings: A Commentary*, The Old Testament Library (Louisville, KY: Westminster John Knox, 2007), 300. See also Fritz, *1 & 2 Kings*, 259–60.

[16] Seow, "2 Kings," 194.

[17] Ibid., 195.

[18] Ibid., 198: "He expected something dramatic, but salvation came to him through the words of a prophet, conveyed to him by a messenger—and it entailed a baptism. This is the way God cleanses people of their afflictions, it seems, not through the dramatic performance of a human healer, but through a simple act of obedience."

[19] Kim, "Reading and Retelling," 55.

[20] Seow, "2 Kings," 195; and Long, *2 Kings*, 72.

[21] Fritz, *1 & 2 Kings*, 260. See also Cohn, *2 Kings*, 38.

[22] Gina Hens-Piazza, a friend and professor of biblical studies at The Jesuit School of Theology of Santa Clara University, in a conversation with the author, May 2015. See also Cohn, *2 Kings*, 37.

[23] "The god Rimmon, who is mentioned by Naaman, appears in Aramaic and Neo-Assyrian sources as a separate deity, although his name is

elsewhere an epithet of the weather god Hadad" (Fritz, *1 & 2 Kings*, 260). See also Brueggemann and Hawkins, "Affirmation of Prophetic Power," 31: "We know nothing about Rimmon, who is never mentioned again anywhere, though there is speculation that he may have been linked to a bigger Syrian god."

[24] Seow, "2 Kings," 195.

[25] "Whereas before his 'conversion,' he denigrates the 'waters of Israel' (v. 12), now he wants Israelite soil, presumably to use for an altar at which to worship YHWH" (Cohn, *2 Kings*, 38).

[26] Seow, "2 Kings," 195.

[27] See Long, *2 Kings*, 73; and Seow, "2 Kings," 196—both of whom use this phrase.

[28] Seow, "2 Kings," 198. See also Walter Brueggemann, "Perpetual Shalom: Elisha's Gift to Naaman," *Christian Century* 129, no. 16 (August 8, 2012): 32: "Elisha expressed no recrimination or rebuke of the ex-leper's intention. He was ready to accept the general's intentions without retaliation. Why? Because Elisha is focused elsewhere. He is not in the business of barter, of making tradeoffs of healing for a continued devotee."

[29] "Elisha responds laconically with a simple formula of dismissal, 'Go in peace,' which suggests that he and God have heard and look favorably on these petitions (see Exod 4:18; Judg 18:6; 1 Sam 1:17; 2 Sam 5:19; cf. Gen 44:17; 1 Sam 25:35b)" (Long, *2 Kings*, 73).

[30] "Getting down from the chariot to meet not Elisha himself, but the servant of Elisha, was a remarkable act of courtesy" (Kim, "Reading and Retelling," 55).

[31] "While Naaman's good reputation preceded him, Gehazi's crime is carried in front of him" (Cohn, *2 Kings*, 41).

[32] "Elisha thus seizes upon Gehazi's evasion and heaps rhetorically exaggerated accusation and punishment upon him, v. 26. If he (Gehazi) has taken money and garments—and, Elisha adds with indignant hyperbole, olive orchards and vineyards, sheep, oxen, servants, amassing goods like some corrupt royal tyrant (Cohn, 182)—then he will also inherit Naaman's leprosy, as will his children" (Long, *2 Kings*, 76). See also Walter Brueggemann, *1 & 2 Kings*, Smyth & Helwys Bible Commentary (Macon, GA: Smyth & Helwys, 2000), 337.

[33] Seow, "2 Kings," 198: "Despite her lowly status and her captivity in a foreign land, she is faithful."

³⁴ Ibid.: "The king of Israel, on the other hand, could only despair, even though salvation was at hand in Samaria." See also Cogan and Tadmor, *II Kings*, 67; and Long, *2 Kings*, 77: "The king nearly blocks the flow of prophetic power by misreading the meaning of Naaman's mission, and implicitly highlights the supernatural currents which move deep within events ('Am I God, to kill and make alive . . . ?' v. 7)."

Chapter 5

¹ Robert Gordon Maccini, "A Reassessment of the Woman at the Well in John 4 in Light of the Samaritan Context," *Journal for the Study of the New Testament* 53, no. 16 (April 1994): 39. See the Cana story in John 2:1-11.

² See P. Kyle McCarter Jr., "Israel," in *HarperCollins Bible Dictionary*, ed. Paul J. Achtemeier, 468 (San Francisco: HarperCollins, 1996). Israel fell in 722 BCE (Before the Common Era).

³ Ibid. See also James D. Purvis, "Samaritans," in *HarperCollins Bible Dictionary*, 963–66.

⁴ See Raymond E. Brown, *The Gospel According to John I–XII*, The Anchor Bible (Garden City, NY: Doubleday, 1966), 170. Also, Joyce Hollyday, *Clothed with the Sun: Biblical Women, Social Justice, and Us* (Louisville, KY: Westminster John Knox, 1994), 210: "Jews generally considered Samaritans impure and inferior, religious apostates. It was no coincidence that Jesus told a parable about a Samaritan helping a wounded Jew at the side of the road to make a point about inclusion and neighborliness. To Jews, the concept of a 'Good Samaritan' was an oxymoron."

⁵ Tracy Kemp Hartman, *Letting the Other Speak: Proclaiming the Stories of Biblical Women* (Lanham, MD: Lexington Books, 2012), 93.

⁶ For more on these betrothal scenes, see Richard B. Hays and Joel B. Green, "The Use of the Old Testament by New Testament Writers," in *Hearing the New Testament: Strategies for Interpretation*, 2nd ed. (Grand Rapids, MI: Eerdmans, 1995), 228. Also, F. Scott Spencer, *Dancing Girls, Loose Ladies, and Women of the Cloth: The Women in Jesus' Life* (New York: Continuum, 2004), 88; and Douglas A. Knight and Amy-Jill Levine, *The Meaning of the Bible: What the Jewish Scriptures and Christian Old Testament Can Teach Us* (New York: HarperCollins, 2011), 55.

⁷ Mary Ann Getty-Sullivan, *Women in the New Testament* (Collegeville, MN: Liturgical Press, 2001), 93. See also Spencer, *Dancing Girls*, 88.

[8] Hartman, *Letting the Other Speak*, 98.

[9] Bonnie Thurston, *Women in the New Testament: Questions and Commentary* (New York: Crossroad, 1998), 84. See also Luise Schottroff, "The Samaritan Woman and the Notion of Sexuality in the Fourth Gospel," in *"What Is John?" Literary and Social Readings of the Fourth Gospel*, vol. 2, ed. Fernando F. Segovia (Atlanta: Society of Biblical Literature, 1998), 165.

[10] This is the only time in the gospels where Jesus is referred to as a Jew. Getty-Sullivan, *Women in the New Testament*, 93–94.

[11] Compare Helen Bruch Pearson, *Do What You Have the Power to Do* (Nashville: Upper Room Books, 1992), 144, to Maccini, "A Reassessment of the Woman at the Well," 38; and Hartman, *Letting the Other Speak*, 97.

[12] Hollyday, *Clothed with the Sun*, 211.

[13] Getty-Sullivan, *Women in the New Testament*, 94.

[14] See, for example, Brown, *The Gospel According to John*, 171; or Teresa Okure, "Jesus and the Samaritan Woman (Jn 4:1-42) in Africa," *Theological Studies* 70, no. 2 (2009): 407.

[15] Schottroff, "The Samaritan Woman and the Notion of Sexuality," 162–63.

[16] Ibid., 162: "For example, the New Testament speaks of the sevenfold levirate marriage of a woman (Mark 12:18-22 part.; cf. Deut 25:5)."

[17] Thurston, *Women in the New Testament*, 85.

[18] Ibid., 84–85. Some scholars suggest the conversation about husbands might refer to the five "false gods" that Jews believed the Samaritans worshiped. In other words, it might all have been an allegory. See also Loring A. Prest, "The Samaritan Woman," *The Bible Today* 30, no. 6 (November 1992): 367–70.

[19] Hartman, *Letting the Other Speak*, 97; and Spencer, *Dancing Girls*, 91.

[20] Prest, "The Samaritan Woman," 370.

[21] Craig Farmer, "Changing Images of the Samaritan Woman in Early Reformed Commentaries on John," *Church History* 65, no. 3 (September 1996): 366–67.

[22] Ibid., 244.

[23] Thurston, *Women in the New Testament*, 84. Also, Hartman, *Letting the Other Speak*, 94: "Recent scholarship has also challenged the long-standing assumption that the woman at the well was ignorant. In Samaria, all children, male and female, received education, so this stereotype is unwarranted."

[24] Okure, "Jesus and the Samaritan Woman," 409.

²⁵ Getty-Sullivan, *Women in the New Testament*, 96.

²⁶ Thurston, *Women in the New Testament*, 91; and Brown, *The Gospel According to John*, 177.

²⁷ Hollyday, *Clothed with the Sun*, 211.

²⁸ Schottroff, "The Samaritan Woman," 167.

²⁹ Brown, *The Gospel According to John*, 173.

³⁰ Ibid. See also Peter J. Scaer, "Jesus and the Woman at the Well: Where Mission Meets Worship," *Concordia Theological Quarterly* 67, no. 1 (January 2003): 9.

³¹ Farmer, "Changing Images," 367. See also Thurston, *Women in the New Testament*, 85: "Just as the male disciples in the Synoptics left nets, boats, and counting houses to follow Jesus, this woman leaves her water jar to return to her village and to share the good news of the Messiah. She is the prototype of apostolic activity."

³² Okure, "Jesus and the Samaritan Woman," 408.

³³ Prest, "The Samaritan Woman," 370–71: "If the Samaritan woman were as unsavory as typically depicted (requiring her to come to the well at odd times to avoid social contact), why did the Samaritan people listen to her? The testimony of any woman in those days was generally considered unreliable." See also Hartman, *Letting the Other Speak*, 98.

³⁴ Brown, *The Gospel According to John*, 175.

³⁵ Okure, "Jesus and the Samaritan Woman," 409. See also John 20.

³⁶ Hartman, *Letting the Other Speak*, 93.

³⁷ Okure, "Jesus and the Samaritan Woman," 408.

³⁸ Farmer, "Changing Images," 366–67.

³⁹ "This woman appears to be without guile or defensiveness, ready and eager to have her own religious hopes fulfilled. When Jesus tells her that she is living with one who is not her husband, she shows no anger. When Jesus says that salvation will come from the Jews, she remains open-minded and attentive" (Getty-Sullivan, *Women in the New Testament*, 96). See also Hartman, *Letting the Other Speak*, 97–98: "It is clear from the woman's questions to Jesus that she was aware of the cultural biases and regulations about ritual purity (she reminded him that he has broken culture codes in speaking with her), that she knew her history and religious heritage, that she was familiar with the theological issues that contributed to the enmity between the Jews and Samaritans, and that she held expectations of a coming prophet and Messiah." Also, Spencer, *Dancing Girls*, 91.

[40] F. Scott Spencer, "Feminist Criticism," in *Hearing the New Testament: Strategies for Interpretation*, 2nd ed., ed. Joel B. Green, 314 (Grand Rapids, MI: Eerdmans, 2010).

Chapter 6

[1] Sharon H. Ringe, "A Gentile Woman's Story," in *Feminist Interpretation of the Bible*, ed. Letty M. Russell, 69 (Philadelphia: Westminster Press, 1985).

[2] Ibid., 81.

[3] Matthew's account is more elaborate, but there's plenty to ponder in Mark's version.

[4] Mainly the scribes and Pharisees. For more on these two groups, see *HarperCollins Bible Dictionary*, ed. Paul J. Achtemeier (San Francisco: HarperCollins, 1996), 980, 841–42.

[5] Joyce Hollyday, *Clothed with the Sun: Biblical Women, Social Justice, and Us* (Louisville, KY: Westminster John Knox, 1994), 204.

[6] Ibid., 269.

[7] Ibid., 205.

[8] Joel Marcus, *Mark 1–8: A New Translation with Introduction and Commentary*, The Anchor Bible (New York: Doubleday, 2000), 462. See also Bonnie Thurston, *Women in the New Testament: Questions and Commentary* (New York: Crossroad, 1998), 72.

[9] Mary Ann Getty-Sullivan, *Women in the New Testament* (Collegeville, MN: Liturgical Press, 2001), 86–87. See also Mark 3:8.

[10] Mary Ann Tolbert, "Mark," in *The Women's Bible Commentary*, ed. Carol A. Newsom and Sharon H. Ringe, 269 (Louisville: Westminster John Knox, 1992).

[11] Ibid., 268.

[12] "She is portrayed as part of the group in that region whose policies and lifestyle would have been a source of suffering for her mostly poorer, rural Jewish neighbors. In so far as that is true, she would have been among those frequently targeted by Jesus' parables and teachings that proclaimed 'good news to the poor'" (Sharon H. Ringe, "A Gentile Woman's Story Revisited: Rereading Mark 7:24-31," in *A Feminist Companion to Mark*, ed. Amy-Jill Levine, 86 [Sheffield: Sheffield Academic Press, 2001]).

[13] Thurston, *Women in the New Testament*, 72.

[14] F. Scott Spencer, *Dancing Girls, Loose Ladies, and Women of the Cloth: The Women in Jesus' Life* (New York: Continuum, 2004), 205–6.

[15] See, for example, David Rhoads, "Jesus and the Syrophoenician Woman in Mark: A Narrative-Critical Study," *Journal of the American Academy of Religion* 62, no. 2 (Summer 1994): 352. Also, Matthew L. Skinner, "'She departed to her house': Another Dimension of the Syrophoenician Mother's Faith in Mark 7:24-30," *Word and World* 26, no. 1 (Winter 2006): 17.

[16] Rhoads, "Jesus and the Syrophoenician Woman in Mark," 356. See also Lynn B.E. Jencks, "Refusing the Syrophoenician Woman: The Disparate Perspectives of Jesus, Mark, and Feminist Critiques," in *Women in the Biblical World*, ed. Elizabeth A. McCabe (Lanham, MD: University Press of America, 2009), 79. Also, Marcus, *Mark 1–8*, 463–64.

[17] Frances Dufton, "The Syrophoenician Woman and her Dogs," *The Expository Times* 100, no. 11 (August 1989): 417.

[18] Ringe, "A Gentile Woman's Story Revisited," 90.

[19] Spencer, *Dancing Girls*, 40.

[20] T. A. Burkill, "The Historical Development of the Story of the Syrophoenician Woman (Mark vii: 24-31)," *Novum Testamentum* 9, no. 3 (1967): 173.

[21] Skinner, "She departed to her house," 16.

[22] Rhoads, "Jesus and the Syrophoenician Woman," 357.

[23] She is, as one writer has observed, "unflinching" (Getty-Sullivan, *Women in the New Testament*, 88).

[24] She "entered the metaphor" (P. Pokorny, "From a Puppy to the Child: Some Problems of Contemporary Biblical Exegesis Demonstrated from Mark 7.24-30/Matt 15.21-8," *New Testament Studies* 41, no. 3 [July 1995]: 328). See also Rhoads, "Jesus and the Syrophoenician Woman," 359: she "extends his proverb." Marcus, *Mark 1–8*, 470: she "accomplishes the rhetorical coup." And Ringe, "A Gentile Woman's Story Revisited," 90: "she turns the offensive label into a harmless one."

[25] Sabine van Den Eynde, "When a Teacher Becomes a Student: The Challenge of the Syrophoenician Woman (Mark 7.24-31)," *Theology*, 103, no. 814 (July/August 2000): 275.

[26] Skinner, "She departed to her house," 17–18.

[27] Rhoads, "Jesus and the Syrophoenician Woman," 360–61. Also, Marcus, *Mark 1–8*, 465.

[28] Skinner, "She departed to her house," 20–21.

[29] Rhoads, "Jesus and the Syrophoenician Woman," 346.

[30] Julien C. H. Smith, "The Construction of Identity in Mark 7:24-30: The Syrophoenician Woman and the Problem of Ethnicity," *Biblical Interpretation* 20, no. 4 (2012): 480.

[31] As did the magi, perhaps? Ranjini Wickramaratne Rebera, "The Syrophoenician Woman: A South Asian Feminist Perspective," in *A Feminist Companion to Mark*, ed. Amy-Jill Levine, 107 (Sheffield: Sheffield Academic Press, 2001).

[32] Rhoads, "Jesus and the Syrophoenician Woman," 360. See also Skinner, "She departed to her house," 21: "She stands as an example of faith, not because she necessarily has a large amount of it, but because she enacts it consistently and deeply. Hers is an insistent, perceptive, and trusting faith. We see it in her beseeching, contending, and traveling."

[33] Rhoads, "Jesus and the Syrophoenician Woman," 361.

[34] Hollyday, *Clothed with the Sun*, 206.

[35] "Five thousand men (andres), all Galilean Jews, it seems, representing the people of Israel (twelve baskets=twelve tribes) (6:30-44)" (Spencer, *Dancing Girls*, 65).

[36] Ibid.: "Four thousand people (tetrakischilioi, not necessarily restricted by gender), multiplying seven loaves into a feast yielding seven baskets of leftovers (70=standard tally of 'the nations' in Genesis 10) (Mark 8:1-10)?"

[37] Surekha Nelavala, "Smart Syrophoenician Woman: A Dalit Feminist Reading of Mark 7:24-31," *The Expository Times* 118, no. 2 (November 2006): 68.

[38] Rebera, "The Syrophoenician Woman," 108.

[39] Rhoads, "Jesus and the Syrophoenician Woman," 371.

[40] van Den Eynde, "When a Teacher Becomes a Student," 276.

[41] Rhoads, "Jesus and the Syrophoenician Woman," 362.

[42] Spencer, *Dancing Girls*, 64.

Afterword

[1] See Miroslav Volf, *Exclusion & Embrace: A Theological Exploration of Identity, Otherness, and Reconciliation* (Nashville: Abingdon Press, 1996), 99–165.

Bibliography

Achtemeier, Paul J., ed. *HarperCollins Bible Dictionary*. San Francisco: HarperCollins, 1996.

Albright, W. F., and C. S. Mann. *Matthew*. The Anchor Bible. Garden City, NY: Doubleday, 1971.

Auld, A. Graeme. *I and II Kings*. The Daily Study Bible Series. Louisville, KY: Westminster John Knox, 1986.

Bird, Phyllis. "The Harlot as Heroine." *Semeia* 46 (1989): 119–39.

Boling, Robert G., and G. Ernest Wright. *Joshua: A New Translation with Notes and Commentary*. The Anchor Bible. Garden City, NY: Doubleday, 1982.

Brown, Raymond E. *The Birth of the Messiah: A Commentary on the Infancy Narratives in the Gospels of Matthew and Luke*. Anchor Bible Reference Library. New York: Doubleday, 1993.

———. *The Gospel According to John I–XII*. The Anchor Bible. Garden City, NY: Doubleday, 1966.

Brueggemann, Walter. *1 & 2 Kings*. Smyth & Helwys Bible Commentary. Macon, GA: Smyth & Helwys, 2000.

———. "Perpetual Shalom: Elisha's Gift to Naaman." *Christian Century* 129, no. 16 (August 8, 2012): 30–33.

Brueggemann, Walter, and Davis Hawkins. "The Affirmation of Prophetic Power and Deconstruction of Royal Authority in the Elisha Narratives." *The Catholic Biblical Quarterly* 76, no. 1 (2014): 58–76.

Bruner, Frederick Dale. *Matthew: A Commentary*. Vol. 1. Grand Rapids, MI: Eerdmans, 1987.

Bruns, J. Edgar. "The Magi Episode in Matthew 2." Miscellanea Biblica. *The Catholic Biblical Quarterly* 23 (1961): 51–54.

Buechner, Frederick. *Peculiar Treasures: A Biblical Who's Who*. New York: HarperOne, 1979.

Burkill, T.A. "The Historical Development of the Story of the Syrophoenician Woman (Mark vii: 24-31)." *Novum Testamentum* 9, no. 3 (1967): 161–77.

Carter, Warren. "Matthew 1-2 and Roman Political Power." Chap. 6 (pp. 77–90) in *New Perspectives on the Nativity*, edited by Jeremy Corley. New York: T&T Clark, 2009.

Clark, Adam. "Hagar the Egyptian: A Womanist Dialogue." *Western Journal of Black Studies* 36, no. 1 (Spring 2012): 48–56.

Coats, G. W. *Genesis*. Grand Rapids, MI: Eerdmans, 1983.

Cogan, Mordechai, and Hayim Tadmor. *II Kings: A New Translation with Introduction and Commentary*. The Anchor Yale Bible, vol. II. New Haven, CT: Yale University Press, 1988.

Cohn, Robert L. *2 Kings*. Berit Olam: Studies in Hebrew Narrative & Poetry, edited by David W. Cotter. Collegeville, MN: Liturgical Press, 2000.

Coote, Robert B. *Joshua*. The New Interpreter's Bible: A Commentary in Twelve Volumes, vol. II. Nashville: Abingdon Press, 1998.

Corley, Jeremy, ed. *New Perspectives on the Nativity*. New York: T&T Clark, 2009.

Creach, Jerome F. D. *Joshua*. Interpretation: A Bible Commentary for Teaching and Preaching. Louisville, KY: Westminster John Knox, 2003.

Crowell, Bradley L. "Good Girl, Bad Girl: Foreign Women of the Deuteronomistic History in Postcolonial Perspective." *Biblical Interpretation* 21, no. 1 (2013): 1–18.

Dufton, Frances. "The Syrophoenician Woman and Her Dogs." *The Expository Times* 100, no. 11 (August 1989): 417.

Exum, J. Cheryl. "Hagar *en Procès*: The Abject in Search of Subjectivity." In *From the Margins 1: Women of the Hebrew Bible and their Afterlives*, edited by Peter S. Hawkins and Lesleigh Cushing Stahlberg, 1–16. Bible in the Modern World. Sheffield: Sheffield Phoenix Press, 2009.

Farmer, Craig. "Changing Images of the Samaritan Woman in Early Reformed Commentaries on John." *Church History* 65, no. 3 (September 1996): 365–75.

Felder, Cain Hope, ed. *Stony the Road We Trod: African American Biblical Interpretation*. Minneapolis: Fortress Press, 1991.

Fewell, Danna Nolan, and David M. Gunn. *Gender, Power, and Promise: The Subject of the Bible's First Story*. Nashville: Abingdon Press, 1993.

Freed, Edwin D. *The Stories of Jesus' Birth: A Critical Introduction*. St. Louis: Chalice Press, 2001.

Fritz, Volkmar. *1 & 2 Kings: A Continental Commentary.* Translated by Anselm Hagedorn. Minneapolis: Fortress Press, 2003.

Frymer-Kensky, Tikva. "Hagar." In *Women in Scripture: A Dictionary of Named and Unnamed Women in the Hebrew Bible, the Apocryphal/Deuterocanonical Books, and the New Testament,* edited by Carol Meyers. Boston: Houghton Mifflin, 2000.

———. *Reading the Women of the Bible: A New Interpretation of Their Stories.* New York: Schocken Books, 2002.

Gallares, Judette A. *Images of Faith: Spirituality of Women in the Old Testament.* Maryknoll, NY: Orbis Books, 1992.

Garland, David E. *Reading Matthew: A Literary and Theological Commentary.* Macon, GA: Smyth & Helwys, 2001.

Getty-Sullivan, Mary Ann. *Women in the New Testament.* Collegeville, MN: Liturgical Press, 2001.

Hare, Douglas R. A. *Matthew.* Interpretation: A Bible Commentary for Teaching and Preaching. Louisville, KY: Westminster John Knox, 1993.

Hartman, Tracy Kemp. *Letting the Other Speak: Proclaiming the Stories of Biblical Women.* Lanham, MD: Lexington Books, 2012.

Hays, Richard B., and Joel B. Green. "The Use of the Old Testament by New Testament Writers." In *Hearing the New Testament: Strategies for Interpretation,* 2nd ed., edited by Joel B. Green. Grand Rapids, MI: Eerdmans, 2010.

Hawkins, Peter S. "God's Trophy Whore." In *From the Margins 1: Women of the Hebrew Bible and their Afterlives,* edited by Peter S. Hawkins and Lesleigh Cushing Stahlberg, 52–70. Bible in the Modern World. Sheffield: Sheffield Phoenix Press, 2009.

Hobbs, T. R. "Naaman." In *The Anchor Bible Dictionary,* vol. 4, edited by David Noel Freedman. New York: Doubleday, 1992.

Hollyday, Joyce. *Clothed with the Sun: Biblical Women, Social Justice, and Us.* Louisville, KY: Westminster John Knox, 1994.

Jencks, Lynn B.E. "Refusing the Syrophoenician Woman: The Disparate Perspectives of Jesus, Mark, and Feminist Critiques." Chap. 6 (pp. 71–86) in *Women in the Biblical World: A Survey of Old and New Testament Perspectives,* vol. 1, edited by Elizabeth A. McCabe. Lanham, MD: University Press of America, 2009.

Kim, Jean Kyoung. "Reading and Retelling Naaman's Story (2 Kings 5)." *Journal for the Study of the Old Testament* 30, no. 1 (2005): 49–61.

Knight, Douglas A., and Amy-Jill Levine. *The Meaning of the Bible: What the Jewish Scriptures and Christian Old Testament Can Teach Us.* New York: HarperCollins, 2011.

Kotansky, Roy. "The Star of the Magi: Lore and Science in Ancient Zoroastrianism, the Greek Papyri, and St. Matthew's Gospel." *Annali di Storia dell'Esegesi* 24, no. 2 (2007): 379–421.

Kselman, John S. "Genesis." In *Harper's Bible Commentary*, rev. ed., edited by James L. Mays. San Francisco: HarperCollins, 2000.

Levine, Amy-Jill, ed., *A Feminist Companion to Mark.* Sheffield: Sheffield Academic Press, 2001.

Long, Burke O. *2 Kings.* Vol. X. The Forms of the Old Testament Literature, edited by Rolf P. Knierim and Gene M. Tucker. Grand Rapids, MI: Eerdmans, 1991.

Lyons, William L. "Rahab in Rehab: Christian Interpretation of the Madame from Jericho." In *Women in the Biblical World: A Survey of Old and New Testament Perspectives*, edited by Elizabeth A. McCabe. Lanham, MD: University Press of America, 2009.

Maccini, Robert Gordon. "A Reassessment of the Woman at the Well in John 4 in Light of the Samaritan Context." *Journal for the Study of the New Testament* 53, no. 16 (April 1994): 35–46.

Marcus, Joel. *Mark 1–8: A New Translation with Introduction and Commentary.* The Anchor Bible. New York: Doubleday, 2000.

Metzger, Bruce M., ed. *The Holy Bible.* New Revised Standard Version. New York: Oxford University Press, 1989.

Murphy, Rosalyn F. T. "Sista-Hoods: Revealing the Meaning in Hagar's Narratives." *Black Theology* 1, no. 1 (April 2012): 77–92.

Nelavala, Surekha. "Smart Syrophoenician Woman: A Dalit Feminist Reading of Mark 7:24-31." *The Expository Times* 118, no. 2 (November 2006): 64–69.

Newsom, Carol A., and Sharon H. Ringe, eds. *The Women's Bible Commentary.* Louisville, KY: Westminster John Knox, 1992.

Nolland, John. *The Gospel of Matthew: A Commentary on the Greek Text.* Grand Rapids, MI: Eerdmans, 2005.

Nowell, Irene. *Women in the Old Testament.* Collegeville, MN: Liturgical Press, 1997.

Nunnally-Cox, Janice. *Foremothers: Women of the Bible.* New York: Seabury Press, 1981.

O'Kane, Martin. "The Artist as Reader of the Bible: Visual Exegesis and the Adoration of the Magi." *Biblical Interpretation* 13, no. 4 (2005): 337–73.

Okure, Teresa. "Jesus and the Samaritan Woman (Jn 4:1-42) in Africa." *Theological Studies* 70, no. 2 (2009): 401–18.

Pearson, Helen Bruch. *Do What You Have the Power to Do*. Nashville: Upper Room Books, 1992.

Pokorny, P. "From a Puppy to the Child: Some Problems of Contemporary Biblical Exegesis Demonstrated from Mark 7.24-30/Matt 15.21-8." *New Testament Studies* 41, no. 3 (July 1995): 321–38.

Powell, Mark Allan. "The Magi as Wise Men: Re-examining a Basic Supposition." *New Testament Studies* 46, no. 1 (January 2000): 1–20.

Prest, Loring A. "The Samaritan Woman." *The Bible Today* 30, no. 6 (November 1992): 367–71.

Rebera, Ranjini Wickramaratne. "The Syrophoenician Woman: A South Asian Feminist Perspective." In *A Feminist Companion to Mark*, edited by Amy-Jill Levine. Sheffield: Sheffield Academic Press, 2001.

Reid, Barbara E. *The Gospel According to Matthew*. New Collegeville Bible Commentary. Collegeville, MN: Liturgical Press, 2005.

Rhoads, David. "Jesus and the Syrophoenician Woman in Mark: A Narrative-Critical Study." *Journal of the American Academy of Religion* 62, no. 2 (Summer 1994): 343–75.

Ringe, Sharon H. "A Gentile Woman's Story." In *Feminist Interpretation of the Bible*, edited by Letty M. Russell. Philadelphia: Westminster Press, 1985.

———. "A Gentile Woman's Story Revisited: Rereading Mark 7:24-31." In *A Feminist Companion to Mark*, edited by Amy-Jill Levine. Sheffield: Sheffield Academic Press, 2001.

Scaer, Peter J. "Jesus and the Woman at the Well: Where Mission Meets Worship." *Concordia Theological Quarterly* 67, no. 1 (January 2003): 3–18.

Schottroff, Luise. "The Samaritan Woman and the Notion of Sexuality in the Fourth Gospel." In *"What Is John?" Literary and Social Readings of the Fourth Gospel*, vol. 2, edited by Fernando F. Segovia. Atlanta, GA: Society of Biblical Literature, 1998.

Seow, Choon-Leong. "2 Kings." *New Interpreter's Bible*, vol. III. Nashville: Abingdon Press, 1999.

Sherwood, Aaron. "A Leader's Misleading and a Prostitute's Profession: A Re-examination of Joshua 2." *Journal for the Study of the Old Testament* 31, no. 1 (2006): 43–61.

Skinner, Matthew L. "'She departed to her house': Another Dimension of the Syrophoenician Mother's Faith in Mark 7:24-30." *Word and World* 26, no. 1 (Winter 2006): 14–21.

Smith, Julien C. H. "The Construction of Identity in Mark 7:24-30: The Syrophoenician Woman and the Problem of Ethnicity." *Biblical Interpretation* 20, no. 4 (2012): 458–81.

Soggin, J. Alberto. *Joshua: A Commentary.* The Old Testament Library. Philadelphia: Westminster Press, 1970.

Speiser, E. A. *Genesis.* The Anchor Bible. New York: Doubleday, 1962.

Spencer, F. Scott. *Dancing Girls, Loose Ladies, and Women of the Cloth: The Women in Jesus' Life.* New York: Continuum, 2004.

———. "Feminist Criticism." In *Hearing the New Testament: Strategies for Interpretation,* 2nd ed., edited by Joel B. Green. Grand Rapids, MI: Eerdmans, 2010.

Spina, Frank Anthony. *The Faith of the Outsider: Exclusion and Inclusion in the Biblical Story.* Grand Rapids, MI: Eerdmans, 2005.

Sweeney, Marvin A., ed. *I & II Kings: A Commentary.* The Old Testament Library. Louisville, KY: Westminster John Knox, 2007.

Tamez, Elsa. "The Woman Who Complicated the History of Salvation." *CrossCurrents* 36, no. 2 (Summer 1986): 129–39.

Thurston, Bonnie. *Women in the New Testament: Questions and Commentary.* New York: Crossroad, 1998.

Tolbert, Mary Ann. "Mark." In *The Women's Bible Commentary,* edited by Carol A. Newsom and Sharon H. Ringe. Louisville, KY: Westminster John Knox, 1992.

Trible, Phyllis. "Ominous Beginnings for a Promise of Blessing." Chap. 2 (pp. 33–70) in *Hagar, Sarah, and Their Children: Jewish, Christian, and Muslim Perspectives,* edited by Phyllis Trible and Letty M. Russell. Louisville, KY: Westminster John Knox, 2006.

———. *Texts of Terror: Literary-Feminist Readings of Biblical Narratives.* Philadelphia: Fortress Press, 1984.

van Den Eynde, Sabine. "When a Teacher Becomes a Student: The Challenge of the Syrophoenician Woman (Mark 7.24-31)." *Theology* 103, no. 814 (July/August 2000): 274–79.

Vawter, Bruce. *A Path through Genesis.* New York: Sheed and Ward, 1956.

Volf, Miroslav. *Exclusion & Embrace: A Theological Exploration of Identity, Otherness, and Reconciliation.* Nashville: Abingdon Press, 1996.

von Rad, Gerhard. *Genesis.* The Old Testament Library. Philadelphia: Westminster John Knox, 1972.

Wansbrough, Henry. "The Infancy Stories of the Gospels since Raymond E. Brown." Chap. 1 (pp. 4–22) in *New Perspectives on the Nativity,* edited by Jeremy Corley. New York: T&T Clark, 2009.

Waters, John W. "Who Was Hagar?" Chap. 3 (pp. 187–205) in *Stony the Road We Trod: African American Biblical Interpretation,* edited by Cain Hope Felder. Minneapolis: Fortress Press, 1991.

Weems, Renita J. "African American Women and the Bible." Chap. 3 (pp. 57–78) in *Stony the Road We Trod: African American Biblical Interpretation,* edited by Cain Hope Felder. Minneapolis: Fortress Press, 1991.

Wray, T. J. *Good Girls, Bad Girls: The Enduring Lessons of Twelve Women of the Old Testament.* Lanham, MD: Rowman & Littlefield, 2008.

Lightning Source UK Ltd.
Milton Keynes UK
UKOW01f2346260917
309928UK00007B/294/P